Edwin Louis Cole

A MAN'S GUIDE TO THE
MAXIMIZED
LIFE

A SIX-WEEK JOURNEY TO GREATER SUCCESS

WHITAKER
HOUSE

A Man's Guide to the Maximized Life:
A Six-Week Journey to Greater Success

Christian Men's Network | P.O. Box 3 | Grapevine, TX 76099
ChristianMensNetwork.com
facebook.com/edwinlouiscole/
facebook.com/ChristianMensNetwork/

ISBN: 978-1-64123-842-7 | eBook ISBN: 978-1-64123-843-4
Printed in the United States of America
© 2022 by Edwin and Nancy Cole Legacy LLC

Whitaker House | 1030 Hunt Valley Circle | New Kensington, PA 15068
www.whitakerhouse.com

Library of Congress Control Number: 2022932728

1 2 3 4 5 6 7 8 9 10 11 ⊔⊔ 29 28 27 26 25 24 23 22

CONTENTS

WEEK 5

WEEK 6

FOREWORD

"While some men build monuments, Ed Cole built men."

What a man does in life becomes history. What he puts into motion becomes his legacy. God's Word promises that if a man trusts in the Lord, his life will never stop producing fruit.

My dad, Edwin Louis Cole, put into motion the intentional discipling of generations of men.

While most of us strive to read books, engage the spirit of the author, and enhance our life's mission, I had the privilege of reading the author before I ever read his books.

My dad lived his life in front of me. Difficulties, victories, tragedies, and joy. Yet, looking back today from a mature age, my takeaway is that he lived life completely in love with Jesus Christ. He never lost the wonder of Jesus' salvation. It permeated his daily walk and talk.

That "spiritual DNA" is now alive in his children and grandchildren, and generations of men who have followed in the footsteps of Ed Cole.

This book is more than a collection of his powerful thoughts. If you read to engage the spirit of the author, this book will be a revelational journey.

Today, around the world millions of men are following Jesus, leading their families, faithful in a Christian community, and changing the future of the world—because this author followed Jesus.

You can, too. God has placed you on earth to bring the love of Christ to the community around you. Your life is so very vital to the expansion of God's grace to others.

The world is transformed when courageous men relentlessly follow Jesus with uncommon devotion.

Be that man.

Live a blessed life. Let your family receive that blessing.

Change the world around you.

Leave a legacy.

> "Blessed are those who trust in the LORD
> and have made the LORD their hope and confidence.
> They are like trees planted along a riverbank,
> with roots that reach deep into the water.
> Such trees are not bothered by the heat
> or worried by long months of drought.
> Their leaves stay green,
> and they never stop producing fruit."
> Jeremiah 17:7–8 NLT

YOUR MAXIMUM POTENTIAL

Canaan land is God's symbol of a man's maximum potential.

It is a basic truth—God has a land of promise and blessing for his people.

It is called Canaan land.

Shangri-La was a fantasy. Canaan land is real.

The meaning of Canaan land applies to your life today. Canaan land has always been God's symbol of mankind's maximized potential. It is the place where God's promises are fulfilled in our lives—the place where God maximizes the potential of his people, both individually and collectively. It affects our spirits, emotions, bodies, marriages, children, and professions.

There, we can reach our maximum potential. There, we can live our maximized life.

In the Old Testament, Canaan land was where God wanted the Israelites to live after he delivered them from their bondage in Egypt. They were to live there in faith, and God would fulfill his promises to them.

A well-known Bible teacher shared a message using a passage of Scripture that had a powerful impact on me some years ago. It was as though it were alive. My heart was stirred as he spoke. I have been dwelling on its importance for men ever since.

Speaking from the New Testament, he listed the five reasons why the Israelites did not get into Canaan land, the land of promise (1 Corinthians 10:6–9). Right after the list, the Scripture states that the Israelites are examples for us. Meaning, this chronicle of sins relates to Israel but has a direct correlation to men today.

What does it mean for you and me?

Like the hapless children of Israel, men today dream of a promised land, a Canaan, where problems can be solved, conflicts ended, and relationships renewed. It is a life of fulfillment, strength, and peace.

But the Israelites failed to reach Canaan for the five reasons listed in 1 Corinthians. They are:

Lust.

Idolatry.

Fornication.

Tempting Christ.

Murmuring.

It is glaringly apparent that these five sins are still the five root causes of men living in unfulfilled potential. They are basic to all humanity.

God wants you to have a Canaan-land marriage, career, family, education, and community.

Yet, most men are not maximized in any of these.

They are men with unfulfilled potential.

That may include you, or someone you know.

I can think about people I have known who failed to reach their "Promised Land" because of sex sins, gossip—which is murmuring—making an idol of money or their career, and the rest. Couples, men, friends, preachers, congressmen, senators, people from every walk of life. Believers and nonbelievers. Sinners and saints.

Canaan land is for all of us—if we can only understand the way to get there.

My desire to help in pointing the way is intense.

I want you to understand that Canaan is a land of promise where God wants you to live by faith today. There, he will fulfill his promises for your life. There, you can reach your maximum potential. You *can* live a maximized life.

THE CHALLENGE

+ The five sins are still the five root causes for men living in unfulfilled potential. They are basic to all humanity.

+ Hearing the word "Canaan," men think of a land from ancient days located across the world. But God still has a Canaan land for us today.

+ Love is the desire to benefit others even at the expense of self because love desires to give. Lust desires to benefit self even at the expense of others because lust desires to get. This is true in the home, in business—in every circumstance.

+ Men committed to the belief that it is desirable and pleasurable to live fast, to beat everyone, and to triumph in multiple sexual encounters, carry the burden of shallow relationships, stalled careers, and failed health.

THE WORD

Now these things occurred as examples to keep us from setting our hearts on evil things as they did. Do not be idolaters, as some of them were; as it is written: "The people sat down to eat and drink and got up to indulge in revelry." We should not commit sexual immorality, as some of them did—and in one day twenty-three thousand of them died. We should not test Christ, as some of them did—and were killed by snakes. And do not grumble, as some of them did—and were killed by the destroying angel. These things happened to them as examples and were written down as warnings for us, on whom the culmination of the ages has come.   1 Corinthians 10:6–11

For I command you today to love the LORD your God, to walk in obedience to him, and to keep his commands, decrees and laws; then you will live and increase, and the LORD your God will bless you in the land you are entering to possess.

Deuteronomy 30:16

2

HOW IMPORTANT IS MONEY?

A man's affection follows his money.

How important is money?

Money represents your life. In return for giving your life at work, you receive money. What you do with your money shows what you do with your life.

Life's values are shown in the use of money. What we value most in life is where we invest most of our money—whether a car, sports, the stock market, a family, or the church.

Our affections follow our money. Jesus said, "For where your treasure is, there your heart will be also" (Matthew 6:21). Where we put our money shows what we love in life.

The world's greatest handbook for learning economic basics is not found in schoolbooks but in the Scriptures. The Bible has a lot to say about the power of money.

"You cannot serve both God and money" (Matthew 6:24) is a principle of life. God must come first. Faith in God *first* makes faith for everything else possible.

"The love of money is the root of all kinds of evil" (1 Timothy 6:10) is another life principle. Money itself is amoral. The morality of money is given to it—by God and by us.

It is not money itself that is evil, but the love or lust for it. The lust for money makes slaves of men.

A man who sees things he wants and begins to lust for them develops an insatiable desire for the money to acquire them. He is guilty of the "lust of the eyes" (1 John 2:16).

Love is easily satisfied. Lust is insatiable. Men lust for things and, as a result, lust for money.

Jesus said, "But seek first the kingdom of God and His righteousness, and all these things shall be added to you" (Matthew 6:33 NKJV). When our faith is placed primarily and fundamentally in God as life's priority, he will add to it all that we need.

Dave's life was a case of misplaced priorities. His sole desire was to be a success. College, business, relationships, everything was keyed to becoming a "somebody."

To succeed financially, Dave desired to climb the corporate ladder. Somehow, every promotion he pursued he missed. As a result, there was constant turmoil in his heart and home. The people he was upset with on the job never heard about it. But those at home—his wife and children who loved him—suffered the effects of his hostilities intended for others.

When things went well at work, he was fine. When they did not, his family bore the brunt of his emotional outbursts and impatience. Their life was a roller coaster, up and down from day to day.

Dave never obtained what he pursued because he put "things" first and expected God to add to them. His life was ruled by circumstances, not by faith. He gauged his success by corporate achievement, while God gauges it by a Christlike character.

Dave eventually recognized he should *seek first the kingdom of God and his righteousness.* He surrendered his professional life and finances to the Lord, and his life finally turned around.

Jesus once said it is harder for a rich man to enter the kingdom of heaven than for a camel to go through the eye of a needle (Mark 10:5). He was referring to men's dependence on money instead of God—our failure to recognize the Lord as the source of our wealth.

Be wise. Set God, not money, as the priority of your heart.

THE CHALLENGE

+ Men tend to see the worth of our manhood in terms of money. But we were meant to fulfill our sense of manhood through a relationship with God *first*.

+ God never meant for us to live without gain. He meant for us to seek the kingdom of God first, and then gain would be added to us.

+ Money is a means to an end—not an end in itself.

THE WORD

No one can serve two masters. Either you will hate the one and love the other, or you will be devoted to the one and despise the other. You cannot serve both God and money.   Matthew 6:24

For the love of money is a root of all *kinds of* evil, for which some have strayed from the faith in their greediness, and pierced themselves through with many sorrows.   1 Timothy 6:10 NKJV

Keep your lives free from the love of money and be content with what you have, because God has said, "Never will I leave you; never will I forsake you."
                    Hebrews 13:5

3

THE STRENGTH OF A MAN

You can pitch personality, but you must build character.

One of my heroes of faith told me something I have never forgotten and have quoted thousands of times: *"When the charm wears off, you have nothing but character left."*

The strength of a man is in his character—his moral fiber.

Strength is always proven by resistance. To prove how strong glue is, place it on two pieces of material, put them together, then try to pull them apart.

The strength of a marriage is determined by the ability to resist forces that try to pull the partners apart.

The strength of a nation, church, or family depends on the character of its members to withstand the pressures to tear it apart.

Most defeated nations and families collapse from within, which makes them vulnerable from without.

The same is true with individuals. And with you.

Your inner strength determines your ability to withstand temptations, accusations, persecutions, seductions, lies, and other pressures that work to weaken you. You must have strength to stand against wrong and for right.

Men and nations are not great by virtue of their wealth, but by the wealth of their virtue.

The world needs strong men with strong character.

Many men spend too much time on the temporal and not enough on the eternal—too much time on building personality, while merely pitching character. It's a perversion of godly principles.

You can pitch personality, but you must build character.

Life is lived on levels and arrived at in stages.

That's why the steps of a righteous man "are ordered by the LORD" (Psalm 37:23 NKJV). Each step advances you to a new level of responsibility, knowledge, or authority and calls for further deepening of your character.

In spiritual growth, there is no retirement age.

Real manhood cannot be found in just a moment's emotional outburst. Neither is real manhood found in the image of physical prowess and good looks. Nor in personality, intelligence, performance, profession, or talent.

Real manhood is found within the heart of a man—the "inner man"—his moral character. The real man exudes character beyond all external devices for the rest of the world to see.

Whatever a man is in private—what he believes, practices, and has built into his character—determines the actions and decisions he makes in public.

Charm is for the instant. Character is constant.

As you become a man of character, you build not on what you can gain from the moment, but on what will benefit you for life.

Out of the heart spring the issues of life (Proverbs 4:23). Moral character, which denotes real manhood, emanates from the inner core of a man's being, his heart. And the man who has revealed that character most completely and consistently is Jesus Christ.

Jesus came to earth as the express image of God. He knew in whose image he was created and who he represented. As such, he was secure in his identity. Because Jesus is "real," men who find themselves in him discover true security in identification with him. He, in turn, begins to reshape them into his perfect image.

Build your character on the foundation of truth. Use faithfulness as its cornerstone. Make righteousness its walls. Then your good character will be known by all.

THE CHALLENGE

+ Trying to develop a godly character apart from God will fail. Developing Christlikeness from a heart turned toward God will cause a man to grow in character and stand for all eternity.

+ Life is composed of our choices, constructed by our words, and revealed by our character.

+ What you believe is the basis for conduct, character, and destiny.

+ God will never ask us to do anything inconsistent with his will, contrary to his character, or in opposition to his Word.

THE WORD

A good name is to be chosen rather than great riches, loving favor rather than silver and gold.

Proverbs 22:1 NKJV

Examine yourselves to see whether you are in the faith; test yourselves.   2 Corinthians 13:5

Stand true to the Lord; act like men; be strong.

1 Corinthians 16:13 TLB

4

THE VALUE OF APPRECIATION

Everything in life appreciates or depreciates.

Everything in life appreciates or depreciates. When something appreciates, it gains in value. When it depreciates, it loses in value.

Homes, cars, land, stocks—all appreciate or depreciate according to the value placed upon them.

Humans also appreciate or depreciate according to the value placed upon them. When you appreciate your wife, she gains in value—in her eyes and in yours. When you depreciate her, she loses in value—in her eyes and in yours.

Years ago, Nancy and I were pastoring a struggling church in Northern California. Actually, everything around me was struggling, me most of all.

We were remodeling the building, making it inviting with a new hardwood floor. In each spare moment, I pounded nails into it to speed the process.

Alone one afternoon, with each blow of the hammer, I pounded out my own frustrations...frustrations toward God; toward my wife, Nancy; toward the struggling congregation; toward myself. I told God exactly how I felt.

"God, you've got to do something! God, you've got to change this situation! You've got to help me! Change these circumstances! Change Nancy! Change the congregation! *God—I need help!*"

Nancy and I were living in only four hundred and twenty square feet with two children, agonizing over every penny, growing more and more frazzled.

God heard my prayer. God answered me.

As I stood there pounding nails, God opened my mind.

He pressed the "rewind" button and began to replay for me excerpts of my own words. He reminded me of what I had been saying about Nancy. Each judgmental attitude. Every demeaning verbal stroke. Each time I had depreciated her with some comment. My constant murmuring.

I loved my wife. Yet, I had fallen into an attitude common to man.

Nancy—because of her convenience—had become the target of my frustration, the object of my humor, and the scapegoat for my failures.

I was stunned and shattered by the revelation. I felt the hot hand of shame against the back of my neck. Then God did something for which I shall ever be grateful. He showed me her graciousness, virtues, loveliness, and beauty of spirit. I saw her as God saw her.

Instantly, I dropped the hammer, lay down on that hard floor, and asked God to forgive me. Deep within my spirit, I cried out to God—but this time altogether differently. I raised my hands toward heaven and lifted my voice.

"God forgive me for my attitude! Forgive me for the way I've regarded my wife! I want to love her! I want to appreciate her—not depreciate her. I receive her as your gift to me! I thank you for her!"

Much later, broken and remodeled, I headed home. I cleaned up and went downtown to pick up a little gift and a simple card.

I got home at dinnertime. I handed Nancy the card and gift, giving her a kiss on the cheek.

"What's this for?" she asked.

"Just because I love you," I told her.

She looked at me a moment, perhaps checking her intuition to make sure of my motivation.

"Really?" she offered tentatively.

"Yes," I answered.

She opened the gift. It was something simple, but she glowed over it, her eyes dancing.

So simple. Yet, life changed that day. Appreciation had begun its work. Depreciation's work was over. Finished.

It was a lasting change. Our relationship—everything—was different.

That's the day I began to refer to Nancy as *"The loveliest lady in the land."*

And she is.

THE CHALLENGE

+ Look your wife in the eyes today and tell her how special she is to you.

+ Do you habitually make jokes about or murmur against your wife? Change—both your words and your heart towards her.

+ If you treat your wife like a servant instead of like a joint-heir, your children will observe it and reflect the same attitude in their actions.

+ The greatest thing a man can do for his children is to love their mother.

+ God doesn't inhabit the gripes, complaints, and criticisms of his people, but their praises (Psalm 22:3 KJV). For God to inhabit your marriage, appreciate and praise your wife.

THE WORD

The LORD has been witness between you and the wife of your youth, with whom you have dealt treacherously; yet she is your companion and your wife by covenant....Therefore take heed to your spirit, and let none deal treacherously with the wife of his youth.

Malachi 2:14–15 NKJV

But at the beginning of creation God "made them male and female." "For this reason a man will leave his father and mother and be united to his wife, and the two will become one flesh." So they are no longer two, but one flesh.   Mark 10:6–8

Be happy, yes, rejoice in the wife of your youth.…Let her love alone fill you with delight.

Proverbs 5:18–19 TLB

5

"YOU'RE THE ONE"

We are committed to what we confess.

"How did you happen to marry your wife?" I asked a man one day.

"She was the sister of a friend of someone I went on a blind date with one time," he shrugged.

Obviously, his destiny.

"Why did you marry your wife?" I asked another.

"I was following a military parade down the street when someone grabbed me and kissed me, and later I married her."

A patriotic partnership if nothing else.

"Why did you marry your spouse?" I asked a young woman.

"I couldn't wait to get away from home," she said. "My parents were unbearable. I married the first man I dated."

I wondered if he knew that.

I've watched couples agonize for hours in counseling sessions before they confront the truth about their motives for marriage. Often, it turns out the marriage commitment is deeply flawed. Either the husband or wife or both do not really believe that their partner was God's choice for them.

The foundation of the marriage then becomes not a solid rock, but rather a quagmire of hurts, misunderstandings, suspicions, resentment, and guilt.

Women were created with a God-given uniqueness. Every woman needs to be unique in her own eyes. Every woman needs to know she is unique to her man.

When that uniqueness is satisfied, a woman becomes a man's wife, best friend, and the completion of his life. When that uniqueness is ignored or stifled, or she believes she is simply lusted after, she becomes just another unfulfilled woman. That's why before engaging in sex women often ask the age-old question, "Do you love me?"

Mechanical sex cannot satisfy the desire for true intimacy.

A man ministers to his wife by giving her assurance.

You assure your wife of your love for her when you tell her she is the one God wants you to have.

We are committed to what we confess.

The marriage vow is a confession that causes commitment. But a lack of commitment is a major issue facing couples today. Many men feel they married too soon or were cornered by circumstances. As a result, they imagine a destiny that might have been.

Likewise, when a woman marries because of pressures, she is often uncertain that her husband is God-given.

In the midst of such uncertainty, spouses will look at others and fantasize. "What would it have been like with her/ with him?"

All of this decomposes the marriage relationship.

Every husband needs to realize that the sacredness of the marriage union is God's highest priority in any marriage. The covenant of marriage is God-ordained. Every man needs to settle in his mind: "She's the one." Having done that, he must confess it—state it out loud—to himself and to her. Such a confession is crucial in affirming your commitment to the marriage.

You minister to your wife when you state that she is the one for you, that she completes your life.

It's her assurance. Her security.

God's love is unconditional, sacrificial, and redemptive. Men in covenant relationship with him through Jesus Christ are to manifest those same Christlike characteristics. This is how a man is to love his wife.

My advice to men the world over has been to tell their wives every day that they love them.

Turn to your wife *today*, look her straight in the eyes and say, "You are God's gift to me. I love you."

THE CHALLENGE

+ The marriage vow is a confession that underlies commitment.

+ A man of God gives his word in marriage and keeps it.

+ You assure your wife of your love for her when you tell her she is the one God wants you to have.

+ Two people can live under the same roof in the same house, share the same bed, eat the same food, and yet be miles apart. Love is the affection that closes the gap.

+ Real men know that love brings intimacy with God and with their wives.

THE WORD

Husbands, love your wives, just as Christ loved the church and gave himself up for her.   Ephesians 5:25

Above all, love each other deeply, because love covers over a multitude of sins.   1 Peter 4:8

Love is patient, love is kind. It does not envy, it does not boast, it is not proud. It does not dishonor others, it is not self-seeking, it is not easily angered, it keeps no record of wrongs. Love does not delight in evil but rejoices with the truth. It always protects, always trusts, always hopes, always perseveres. Love never fails.   1 Corinthians 13:4–8

6

FATHERHOOD: A NOBLE CALLING

Trust funds can never be a substitute for a fund of trust.

Men have long striven to give their children "a better life than I had."

We establish trusts and college funds. We pull strings behind the scenes to get jobs for our children. We pave the way however we can.

But—trust funds can never be a substitute for a fund of trust.

I have been far from the perfect parent. But once I began to make Nancy my joint-heir, to appreciate rather than depreciate her, parenting became a less tumultuous effort.

Parenting is life's greatest art form.

Life and death are in our decisions.

My daughter Lois marched through law school and passed the bar with a flourish. Today, Lois is a deeply rooted Christian wife and mother and a successful attorney. But there was a day when Lois's future hinged on my willingness to make the right decision.

For five years, I had been the president of a denominational men's organization, with five thousand men and four thousand boys under my leadership. The job required ceaseless travel and absences from home.

Nancy welcomed me home one day with a tense expression on her face. Lois seemed to be slipping away. She was a popular girl, always in the social limelight. But now she was letting peer pressure affect her attitude and behavior. Her new friends did not hold to the same standards of Christian life that we held in our home.

I looked at my job. I loved it. The nationwide travel and speaking engagements suited me fine. And yet my daughter needed a father.

Nancy and I agreed that it would be best if I were home more consistently. I resigned from my position, accepted the pastorate of a church, and settled in to become more of a full-time father. It was a quality decision. And the right one.

The solution to family problems, in God's order for the family, is to begin with the father. It is a rare family these days where the man exercises leadership in solving family problems. Men abdicate this part of their manhood.

Today's father thinks too often that fathering is paying the bills, providing a home and education, administering an occasional lecture, and, at various times, being the disciplinarian.

But fathering is a comprehensive task. It means thinking, studying, monitoring, recommending, influencing, and loving. It means pointing your children to Jesus Christ.

God has planned for someone to take charge in your home. *It is you.*

Active fathers who lead their children into a strong relationship with God and family maximize their own manhood. Leading your family in righteousness is your prime responsibility and priestly ministry. To abandon it for personal pleasure, forfeit it through moral cowardice, or shirk it because of irresponsibility is wrong.

The true legacy of a father is in the spirit he gives his children.

The apostle Paul gave the premise for a good father when he said, "Follow my example, as I follow the example of Christ" (1 Corinthians 11:1). The pattern for fathering is to "train up a child in the way he should go" (Proverbs 22:6 KJV, NKJV).

Children may not always listen to you, but they will always imitate you. The example set is not in the words that are spoken but in the deeds that are done.

A father's noblest action is giving himself to his children, and to God.

THE CHALLENGE

+ A father's responsibility is to provide intimacy, discipline, love, and value for his family.

+ The legacy of a father is the character he instills in his sons and daughters.

+ It is not the father's responsibility to make all his children's decisions for them but to let them see him make his.

+ Be Christlike in all you do with your family. They need it, society needs it, your family needs it, and the kingdom of God needs it.

THE WORD

Teach [the Scriptures] to your children, talking about them when you sit at home and when you walk along the road, when you lie down and when you get up.

Deuteronomy 11:19

As a father has compassion on his children, so the LORD has compassion on those who fear him.

Psalm 103:13

Start children off on the way they should go, and even when they are old they will not turn from it.

Proverbs 22:6

The father of a righteous child has great joy; a man who fathers a wise son rejoices in him.

Proverbs 23:24

7

COURAGE

Courage is a requirement of leadership.

I was the general manager of a television station when it came time to reduce personnel for economic reasons. My son Paul was a program producer there, but others had more seniority. A choice had to be made. I called Paul in to tell him what was happening. After hearing me out, he looked at me, then said something that made me realize what a real man he had become.

"Dad, let me go. I'll make it on my own."

He did.

It was hard for both of us, requiring courage, but as I look back at it, that is the day that I realized his manhood.

"Be of good courage" is a scriptural refrain. "Take courage," is the command angels often used as salutations. "Be of good cheer" really means to "be of good courage."

Courage is the virtue, quality, or attribute of life that enables a man to face disapproval, persecution, fear, failure, and even death with a real manliness.

John Kennedy made a name for himself before ever becoming president with his book *Profiles in Courage*. And yet profiles in courage are nothing new—not after you have read about Abraham, Joshua, Moses, David, Paul, and the other "heroes of faith" in the Bible. Their exploits were such that "the world was not worthy of them" (Hebrews 11:38).

Scripture recounts Joseph living in Potiphar's house and being tempted by Potiphar's wife, who tried to seduce him. Joseph rebuked her, saying, "How then can I do this great wickedness, and sin against God?" (Genesis 39:9 NKJV). The honor of God was the criteria of his life. That's manliness.

It takes courage to be a man.

Much of the modern church has failed to inspire, or require, courage in its men. Courage, not just faith, is required of men.

You must add courage to your faith.

Nehemiah, the three Hebrew children, Daniel—Scripture is replete with these who added courage to their faith.

John the Baptist added courage to his faith and, having rebuked the king, was beheaded. But John knew the principle, as have others since then: *There are some things in life more important than life itself.*

A plane crashes into the Potomac. Rescue workers race to save the drowning victims, but one woman cannot be reached. A bystander throws off his jacket and jumps into the icy river to save her. The next day he is heralded across the country as a hero. When asked later what motivated his bravery, he simply said that, at the spur of the moment, he saw a need, and he knew he had to help.

Courage is acting in a moment of time on a need greater than self.

There are really no split-second decisions. Every decision you make as a man is based on a lifetime of decisions which either enhanced or diminished your character. And your character is what determines your courage.

Courage is necessary to change.

Many men will change wives, children, businesses—anything, rather than change themselves. Real men have the courage to face reality and change.

Children need fathers of good courage.

Young men need heroes—a Joshua kind of dad who will shout, "As for me and my house, we will serve the LORD" (Joshua 24:15 NKJV). They need Daniels who will face the legal lions of our day and shut their mouths from speaking against God.

It takes courage to stand by your convictions.

It takes courage to be a man.

Take courage.

THE CHALLENGE

+ Truth, honor, integrity—all require courage.

+ The result of prayer in private will be a life of boldness and courage in public.

+ It takes courage to resist the pressure of peers—courage to hold to your convictions.

+ There are some things in life more important than life itself.

+ Courage is acting in a moment of time on a need greater than self.

THE WORD

Be on your guard; stand firm in the faith; be [men of courage]; be strong. Do everything in love.

1 Corinthians 16:13–14

For this very reason, giving all diligence, add to your faith virtue [manliness, courage], to virtue knowledge, to knowledge self-control, to self-control perseverance, to perseverance godliness, to godliness brotherly kindness, and to brotherly kindness love.

2 Peter 1:5–7 NKJV

Have I not commanded you? Be strong and courageous. Do not be afraid; do not be discouraged, for the LORD your God will be with you wherever you go.

Joshua 1:9

8

A HERO'S DREAM

Heroes are men who act in a moment of time on
a need greater than self.

All men dream of being lauded as heroes.

But few men know what it takes or how to get there.

God created men to be leaders and heroes. That's why every man dreams of himself in a heroic act:

It's the bottom of the ninth in the seventh game of the World Series. Your team is behind with the score five to two. The bases are loaded, you're at bat, and the count is three balls and two strikes. You have only one more pitch to hit, and you zing it over the fence for a grand slam and run the bases into history.

You are a dedicated doctor, cutting through the harrowing jungle with medicine to rescue a village of sick and starving children.

Of such stuff are heroic fantasies created.

Heroes are men who act in a moment of time on a need greater than self.

Men dream of themselves as heroes. Women dream of men as heroes. Children see men as heroes.

Yet far from living strong, heroic lives, today's men are scrambling to regain a sense of manhood that seems to have vanished. Some intangible force has emasculated true manhood—that quality that lingers in history books and biographies. The more men try to grasp it, the more fleeting it seems, and the more frustrated they become.

Masses of men have lost what it means to be a man, a hero, a leader. A moral pollution is taking its toll. Manhood is disintegrating before our eyes.

There is a great need for men to understand what is happening and to do something about it.

Things are not as God intended.

God created this whole thing—manhood—including you and me. By his active presence, he sustains it all. Through our relationship with Jesus Christ, God maximizes a man.

The concept of true manhood was brought home to me by my mentor, a "prince of the pulpit." He survived a childhood spinal injury and stood less than five feet tall. Yet Dr. C. E. Britton was a man's man and one of the finest men I have ever known. He never experienced a night without pain, yet he faithfully and marvelously discipled tremendous men of God and watched them establish great worldwide ministries.

Dr. Britton was ministering one Sunday morning from Luke chapter 13. He pointed out that just as the farmer expects figs under the leaves of his fig trees, so God expects fruit from our lives. The result, the product of the inner working of God in our lives, will be visible fruit. And since we belong to him, God has a right to expect fruit.

That fruit is *manhood*.

Whatever God plants, he wants it to produce.

Orange trees produce oranges. Grapevines produce grapes. Fig trees produce figs. You do not get lemons from grapevines, nor figs from an orange tree.

God created us as men and planted his Spirit within us. He expects to reap the fruit of manhood.

Men—Leaders—Heroes.

Today, more than ever before, we need to recognize how God originally made us and earnestly endeavor to let God recreate our manhood in the image of Christ.

It's the reason we must allow God to produce the fruit of manhood in our lives.

THE CHALLENGE

+ Heroes are men who act in a moment of time on a need greater than self.

+ For men to be men once again, we must regain the spirit of manhood in virility and integrity, the power of manhood in productivity and leadership, the conviction of manhood in resolve and moral excellence.

+ Manhood is in spirit. It has nothing to do with physical size, but everything to do with character.

+ Men were born to be leaders, champions, heroes.

THE WORD

You did not choose Me, but I chose you and appointed you that you should go and bear fruit, and that your fruit should remain.   John 15:16 NKJV

I want the company of the godly men and women in the land; they are the true nobility.   Psalm 16:3 TLB

I will make the godly of the land my heroes and invite them to my home.   Psalm 101:6 TLB

9

IT'S HOW YOU HANDLE IT

You can tell a man's character better by his use of money
than by his way of worship.

Money is life's support system.

Money is a magnifier—it exposes character. Money is an indicator—it shows priorities. Money is a propagator—it shows vision.

Money never leaves you where it found you. Depending on what you do with it, money can provide a blessing or a curse. Money becomes an issue when men worship what money can do.

Money is to be our servant. Worry and debt make a man a servant to money. Debt is a bondage to any man. Living our lives to pay our debts is slavery, not freedom.

It's been said that "too many men buy things they don't need with money they don't have to impress people they don't like." We live in a credit-card society. Spend now, pay later. Instant gratification is the rule of the day.

Your life is worth too much to spend it for debt payments. We were born free, and God wants us to live free, a debtor to no man (Romans 13:8).

Men tend to worry with money and without it. Worry and debt both borrow against tomorrow. God does not want us to be so wrapped up with our tomorrows that we are unresponsive to the Word of God in our todays.

Money issues are top stress points between a husband and wife. The lack of knowledge in the right use of money has killed more than one marriage and crippled thousands of others.

When making decisions about finances or considering a budget, a husband and wife must be in agreement. A man who makes financial decisions unilaterally, without considering his wife's input, puts a terrible strain on a marriage.

Tithing is necessary because it is only for those who tithe that God promises to rebuke the devourer (Malachi 3:10–11 NKJV). Tithing is evidence of faith and trust in God and his Word.

Once you—and your wife, if you're married—get in agreement, get out of debt, and become tithers to conquer a financial crisis or become better stewards, these steps will release the power of God to work in your life.

These ten practical principles summarize the proper ways of handling money:

1. Recognize that God is your Source.

2. Seek God first in everything.

3. Get out of debt.

4. Live within your means.

5. If married, don't make unilateral financial decisions.

6. Start where you are with what you have.

7. Recognize that tithing is a basic, visible evidence of faith.

8. Be generous with God—and with others.

9. Know that to obey God today is to trust Him for tomorrow.

10. Keep adequate records.

Become wise in handling money.

Become the master of your finances, not the servant.

Be generous. God is generous. He lavishes his grace on us. Be generous with God, with your family, with others.

THE CHALLENGE

+ Families are destroyed from mishandled money—there is stress in having too much money, and also in not having enough.

+ The proper use of money produces prosperity.

+ Wise investments lead to financial security and stability.

+ Too many men buy things they don't need with money they don't have to impress people they don't like.

THE WORD

"Bring all the tithes into the storehouse, that there may be food in My house, and try [test] Me now in this," says the Lord of hosts, "if I will not open for you the windows of heaven and pour out for you such blessing that there will not be room enough to receive it. And I will rebuke the devourer for your sakes...."

Malachi 3:10–11 NKJV

Owe no one anything except to love one another, for he who loves another has fulfilled the law.

Romans 13:8 NKJV

The rich rule over the poor, and the borrower is slave to the lender. Proverbs 22:7

The LORD will give grace and glory; no good thing will He withhold from those who walk uprightly.

Psalm 84:11 NKJV

10

MOSES AND THE TEN INVITATIONS

We are not "invited" to obey God.

As a guest on a Christian talk show, I was explaining to the host and cohost that the Lord had impressed me to *command* men to repent.

There was a pause for a station break. The cohost leaned toward me and, with our microphones dead, said, "No, no, no! We *command* Christians, but *invite* sinners."

"No, no, no," I responded, "Acts seventeen says that God 'now commands all men everywhere to repent'" (Acts 17:30 NKJV).

God commands us to repent.

There is a key difference between a command and an invitation.

If I give you an invitation, you have an option. You can either receive it or reject it. But if I command you, you have no option. You either obey or rebel. In the psychologizing of our gospel in modern church life, we have been taught to "invite" people to accept Jesus. Given the option, they reject it.

God didn't take Moses up on the mountain and give him a list of "Ten Invitations." God gave *commandments*.

God's commandments are absolutes.

God commands confession.

We are to confess sin. "If we confess our sins, he is faithful and just to forgive us our sins, and to cleanse us from all unrighteousness" (1 John 1:9 KJV). We are to confess Christ and his righteousness. "Confess with your mouth the Lord Jesus.... For...with the mouth confession is made unto salvation" (Romans 10:9–10 NKJV).

God even commands us to love. According to God, love is not a feeling. Love centers in the will. That is why love can be commanded and why God can command love.

I was standing in front of an auditorium at the end of a meeting when an exuberant couple greeted me. Arms interlocked, occasionally smiling at each other, the husband told me of the miracle in their lives.

"We are a miracle marriage," he said. "For years, I made my wife's life a hell on earth. Unfaithful, inconsiderate, dictatorial, selfish—all I wanted was for her to do what was necessary for me to enjoy life.

"Oh, we went to church, and everyone saw us as a fine family—but no one knew me privately. Not even she did. All she knew was that she had come to the end of her rope and was leaving me. That's when I awoke to how and what I was.

"Then I changed. Or, rather, the Lord Jesus Christ changed me. When I confessed what I was and how I was living, and genuinely repented with godly sorrow, God heard my prayer and changed me.

"But by then, my wife didn't want me. She said whatever love she had was dead, and she could never love me again. I knew she believed that, but I believed in a God of miracles. So I prayed and began to love her in my heart, and to court her as I had at the first. Only this time, the Lord helped me. Eventually, she agreed to try the marriage again.

"Together we began to pray, talk—and I loved her. You know, today we love each other as we never did before. I have such a genuine appreciation for God. He really can make what is dead to live again. You tell the world that if God did it for us, he can do it for them."

We are not *invited* to obey God.

We are *commanded* to obey.

When a man obeys God, he maximizes his manhood.

THE CHALLENGE

+ The Ten Commandments have never been replaced as the moral basis upon which society rests.

+ Unconfessed sin is unforgiven sin.

+ Men and women tell me of their inability to love, saying, "I can't love anymore." Not true.

+ By yielding your will to the will of God and allowing the Holy Spirit to bring God's love into your relationship, you can love. Why? Because God doesn't command something that can't be done.

THE WORD

Whoever has my commands and keeps them is the one who loves me.   John 14:21

Love one another.   John 15:12 NKJV

Husbands, love your wives, just as Christ loved the church and gave himself up for her.   Ephesians 5:25

My command is this: Love each other as I have loved you.   John 15:12

"WILL YOU BE A MAN?"

To be strong, a man must conquer himself.

"All I want him to do is be a man. Just a man."

I sat up straight in that stuffy conference room and looked at her, then at him. It was a fair desire on her part. Her husband had exercised little leadership in the home. Because of that, his sons had lost all respect for him.

Acting as both disciplinarian and comforter for each of the children, as well as working full-time, the wife was wearied with her responsibilities. Neither was there any spontaneity in their life, maritally, recreationally, or sexually. She wanted spice. He gave grits. She wanted something romantic and stimulating. He offered repetition and boredom.

Now, she had made her case. She had declared her desires.

"All I want him to do is just be a man."

I looked squarely at him. "You heard her," I said. "She wants a man. Can you give her one? She wants you."

He looked at me for a moment or two, eyeball to eyeball, then looked away. He gazed up at the ceiling for a long, long time. The silence was like soil—growing awkwardness, flowering into tension. I remembered to let him speak first. It was up to him to answer.

He had never been forced to decide before. His parents had always answered for him. Then his wife compensated for him both in public and private, letting him hide behind her answers. But after two decades of schooling, marriage, children, and work, this man was going to have to answer for himself.

There are two great questions every man must give an answer to.

The first and most important in all of life is, "What will you do with Jesus?"

The second is, "Will you be a man?"

Here was a man on the brink. His answer required manhood. Honesty, truthfulness, faith, humility, courage, love, grace—all the characteristics of manhood were being called forth from the depths of his character. Here in the presence of his wife, his God, and his minister, he had to face the question, "Will you be a man?"

His eyes swung down from the ceiling and focused slowly on his wife's face. They sat not just eye to eye and face to face, but soul to soul. The words were only a faint whisper when they finally came, but it was like thunder in that room.

"I'll try."

Her face filled with happiness, tears sprang up, and she reached for him to embrace him. His answer had come from the depths of his soul, not lightly, but with the weightiness of his entire life. He had considered the question and declared his decision.

Manhood is not magic. No magic wand can produce it instantly. It is built, layer upon layer, line upon line, precept upon precept, decision upon decision.

It is the longing of every woman to have a man with character in the house. It is the need of every child to have a father at the helm. It is the crying need of every church to have real men at work in its ministry. You can derive spirituality from women in the church, but you get strength from the men. Same in a home and in a nation. Churches, homes, and nations are only as strong as their men.

Man has conquered the mountains, the oceans, and even outer space. But the greatest achievement of all is when man conquers himself.

THE CHALLENGE

+ To be strong, a man must conquer himself.

+ God doesn't expect men to be angels. He only expects us to be men.

+ When a man learns and lives according to principles, he is going to find elements of life that make for success.

+ Every man lives to the level of his faith.

THE WORD

Watch...stand fast in the faith, [act] like men, be strong.　　　　　　　　1 Corinthians 16:13 KJV

[Better is] he who rules his spirit than he who takes a city.　　　　　　　　Proverbs 16:32 NKJV

12

CHANGE FROM THE TOP

Change is not change until it is change.

Change always comes by revelation from the top.

If it doesn't, it will come by revolution from the bottom.

Al was a troubleshooter for failing businesses. His clients were companies on the verge of disaster. He was never called until a company was in crisis. By then, the corporate officers were usually ready to listen and swallow the bitter pill of truth. Survival depended on change.

There was almost always a pattern to these corporate nightmares. *Personnel is always the problem, and personnel is always the solution.* The solution almost always originated from the personnel at the top.

Al told me, "No company that is sick can be healed and made financially healthy unless the people at the top are willing to change." Almost without exception, the problems were caused by chief executive officers. "Unless they are willing to change, there is no hope," Al said.

In presenting his analysis and making his recommendations, Al said that invariably it included a change in the leadership. A change in method, motive, attitude, relationships, or, at times, even in the person's lifestyle, or else dismissal.

That principle is applicable to every area of human life, including the family.

The man needs to change so his family can change.

Intention to change is not change. Talking about changing, pledging it, making resolutions concerning it—none of these is change. None of that will heal a hurting home.

The man is the head of the house: *change is to start with him* (Ephesians 5:23).

God doesn't want to change your personality, your drive, or your ego. God expects only one thing from you—manhood.

Manhood isn't talked, it's lived.

Years ago, my family and I lived in the Bay Area of Northern California. On the first Sunday morning in our new pastorate, our congregation consisted of one woman and her baby. Obviously, there was little income. Some days we found ourselves eating oatmeal for breakfast, lunch, and dinner. Slowly, the church grew.

John and his family came, liked us, and stayed. He worked for the airlines and was moderately successful financially. But John was a talker rather than a doer.

I'll never forget one Sunday when he said, "Pastor, if I had a million dollars, I'd give you a tithe. Or if I had a thousand, I'd give you a hundred." I said nothing, but I thought, *Brother, if you had ten, a dollar would help right now.*

He was always going to do things, or change his ways, but he never did. John deceived himself by thinking that talking about it was doing it.

Men tell their wives the same kinds of things. "Once we have the money, I'll take you out." Or a father will say to his child, "When I get some time off work, I'll play ball with you." Yet the same man has time for television and money enough not to pack a lunch.

Change is not change until it is change.

I saw John again thirty years later. Still no change. His value to his family and to God never changed either. Always a talker and not a doer. That's not the manhood God wants from us. To change, the heart of man must change through the love of God.

Do you sense your need for change? You're the man—you change, then your family will.

Giving is not giving until it's given.

Faith is not faith until it's action.

THE CHALLENGE

+ Most people judge others by their *actions* and themselves by their *intentions*.

+ A man is sensitive to his need for change, but rather than asking God to change his heart, he changes jobs or even his marriage, and the old habits remain.

+ Couples sense the need for change, but rather than changing in heart or mind, they simply change houses or jobs, and their problems remain.

+ Continuing to do the same things in the same way will always get the same results. To change your results in life, change your practices in life.

THE WORD

Therefore, if anyone is in Christ, the new creation has come: the old has gone, the new is here!

2 Corinthians 5:17

A person may think their own ways are right, but the LORD weighs the heart.

Proverbs 21:2

Do not merely listen to the word, and so deceive yourselves. Do what it says.

James 1:22

Let us not love with words or speech but with actions and in truth.

1 John 3:18

13

FATHERS WITH BLENDED FAMILIES

You are never too young to be taught and never too old to teach.

I was ministering at an all-day Christian Men's event in Tulsa, Oklahoma. Allen brought his fifteen-year-old son to the men's meeting to spend the day with him. At one point, we asked men who wanted to make things right with God to come to the front.

As I saw Allen Jr. standing with his father near the stage, so intensely serious, I asked why he came.

"Because I wanted God to forgive me for being mad at him for taking away my mother," he answered. His mom had died just a few years earlier.

His admission was genuine and meaningful. In a spontaneous gesture to confirm his manhood, we gave him some money to take the family to dinner the next day to tell them what God had done in his life. He chose the restaurant, asked the blessing, and told the waiter he'd be responsible for the bill.

During dinner, Allen Jr. told his family what happened the day before and asked his stepmother to forgive him for the way he had acted toward her. He had invited her parents to join them, and now his step-grandfather stood, came around to him, and hugged the young man.

By this time, most at the table were crying—his sisters, whose lives had been so tragically affected by the loss of their mother and emotionally affected by their brother's resistance to the new stepmother; his father, who had struggled to bridge the gulf between stepmother and son; his step-grandparents, who had watched in sadness as their daughter struggled to blend two families.

As the family cried, forgave, and hugged, diners at other tables listened in and began to cry with them. "I'm so proud of you," said a stranger who came to their table to hug Allen Jr.

An incredible, wonderful work of reconciliation and family unity took place that Sunday at dinner. One young man's forgiveness, brought through the tearful prayers of his parents, affected the lives of others around him immediately and who knows how many more in the years to come.

You're never too young to be taught and never too old to teach.

Hearing from God doesn't depend on age but on relationship.

Blended families and stepparents need extra encouragement on the challenges of parenting. Being a stepfather can require more grace and wisdom than being a natural father because a stepfather must earn the right of authority, whereas the natural father has it birthed into the family. The same is true for stepmothers.

A principle Jesus gave is vital for a stepfather and the children he has gained by marriage: "If you have not been faithful in what is another man's, who will give you what is your own?" (Luke 16:12 NKJV).

In one of our Phoenix events, a man stood to his feet and said, "I could never understand why I was having problems with my stepchildren that I did not have with my own. When I heard that Scripture verse from Luke, it hit me that I have not been as faithful to my stepchildren as I have to my own children—so, beginning tomorrow, there will be no difference between any children."

Every man there stood and cheered.

THE CHALLENGE

+ Any male can conceive a child, but only a man can father a child.

+ Our responsibility is to raise trustworthy children who respect and admire their parents.

+ Stepparents must be especially strong to cope with the attitudes of children when they are suffering dislocation, rejection, and identity crises.

+ As God parents us, so we parent the children he entrusts to our care.

+ No man has the right to talk to his children about God until he has talked to God about his children.

THE WORD

Don't let anyone think little of you because you are young. Be their ideal; let them follow the way you teach and live; be a pattern for them in your love, your faith, and your clean thoughts.   1 Timothy 4:12 TLB

Similarly, encourage the young men to be self-controlled. In everything set them an example by doing what is good. In your teaching show integrity, seriousness and soundness of speech.   Titus 2:6–8

Children, obey your parents in everything, for this pleases the Lord.   Colossians 3:20

14

MAXIMUM SENTENCE

Be restored to a right relationship with God.

I was on a nonstop flight from Los Angeles to Eugene, Oregon, to a men's retreat in the snowy mountains of west central Oregon.

Men.

I knew that they were gathering to hear something worthwhile, something life changing, something they could take back to their homes and their offices, their shops, and their hunting trips. They wanted something that would help them reach the maximum in their manhood.

God was doing something in my spirit on that plane. There was a weightiness, a sobriety, and a heaviness that would not go away.

I took out a pen. I was aware that God's Spirit was inspiring me as I wrote in my notebook.

Finished, I looked at what I had written.

The sentence was one I had never seen before, nor had I ever said anything like it. A sentence of such pungency that I stared at it for a long time, wondering when, where, or to whom it would be given. My spirit suddenly leaped within me, for I knew it was for that night, those men, that retreat.

It was too powerful for me, too bold. But this was God.

I knew I would have to declare it. Command it. Aloud. Publicly. With authority. That night—to those men.

Without God's power, it could be terrible. With God's confirmation, it could be glorious. Bringing liberty.

That evening in Oregon, there was no doubt. No indecision.

As I stood before the unsuspecting crowd of men, I felt an accelerating sense of excitement. We stood together and prayed. Then, before they could sit down, I looked them in the eye and gave them God's command:

"If you are here tonight and committing adultery, fornication, homosexuality, incest, or habitual masturbation; indulging in pornography; gratifying yourself with sexual fantasies; or any other kind of sex sin, I command you in the name of Jesus Christ to repent and be restored to a right relationship with God the Father by being reconciled through Jesus Christ and the power of the Holy Spirit."

The room fell silent for a split second. Those words, scribbled on a simple notepad a few hours before, now cut through the air like an electric shock.

With a single explosive motion, the men's hands shot into the air, and they began crying out in praise and worship to God. The Holy Spirit filled that chapel in the mountains, bringing a remarkable response to a savagely honest question.

These men—businessmen, preachers, laborers, young and old—had craved direction. They had longed for leadership. They had sought God's voice—no matter how stern. They had been crying out for a change in their lives, an end to questionings and wanderings.

Two hundred and sixty-five men ran toward the front of that chapel and began to repent of their sins with an earnest desire to be fulfilled in their potential as men of God. Some wept aloud.

Wall-to-wall men standing before God. Not one man went away untouched or unchanged.

As you read this, I make the same command to you. If you are bound by any of those sins, make this the time for repentance and restoration. Let God do the same thing in you at this very moment as he did in the hearts of those men that night. Repent and receive his forgiveness.

God wants you to be the man you've always wanted to be.

He will give you the power to do it.

THE CHALLENGE

+ All sin promises to serve and please but only desires to enslave and dominate.

+ God's power can change you and cause you to grow in spirit when you repent and surrender your sins to him.

+ God's love is tough enough to continue forgiving, to continue loving.

+ Fulfill your potential as a man. Take a major step in your journey to a maximized life.

+ God's greatest gift to us is the forgiveness of our sins through Jesus Christ.

THE WORD

Everyone who believes in him [Jesus] receives forgiveness of sins through his name.   Acts 10:43

If we confess our sins, he is faithful and just and will forgive us our sins and purify us from all unrighteousness.   1 John 1:9

So overflowing is his kindness toward us that he took away all our sins through the blood of his Son, by whom we are saved.   Ephesians 1:7 TLB

15

THE BIG FIVE

God calls us to enter the place of rest, blessing,
success, ability, and authority.

The sins that kept the Israelites out of Canaan still keep men out today. They are:

Lust: This lust is not necessarily limited to sexual lust. This is a lust that is determined to satisfy self at the expense of God and others. It's the preoccupation with what self wants in every area of life.

Love is of God, and true love is always giving. God's love desires to satisfy the object of his love. "For God so loved the world that he gave his one and only Son" (John 3:16). God *is* love. Love gives.

Lust wants to *get*. It is basically selfish.

Love gives; lust gets.

The Israelites craved what they had in Egypt. They were lovers of pleasure more than lovers of God.

Idolatry: Idolatry is a value system that we create in which we esteem something to be more worthy of our devotion than our devotion to God.

Power, prestige, education, money, business, religion, popularity, ego, pornography—all these can become idols. Some men worship at the shrine of their businesses, others at temples of recreation and sports. Still others may bow at the sounds of an electronic cashier or addictive technology. For some Christians, even their ministry can become an idol.

Idolatry keeps men from being maximized in their potential—personally, maritally, professionally, spiritually.

Fornication: This includes every kind of sex sin. Sin is still sin. No matter how you spell it.

Pornography and fornication are popular, and sexual promiscuity is acceptable everywhere today—except in the Bible.

Many men, who in many areas of their life develop the potential of their manhood, are limited because of their sex sins. Both single and married men—young and old—are subject to the desires, appetites, passions, and temptations that take their toll and prohibit them from becoming what God intends them to be.

When the men of Israel committed fornication, they died in the wilderness, never seeing Canaan. Men still die in their wilderness, bogged down in a moral morass, missing God's best for their lives.

It wasn't God's plan then or now.

Tempting Christ: Tempting Christ is demanding that God do what is contrary to his will or inconsistent with his character. When the crowds demanded that Christ come down from the cross, that was "tempting" him. Today, men still do the same by demanding that God provide some way of salvation other than the cross.

Lying and cheating in business and demanding that God bless and prosper it is tempting Christ. Believers wanting to enjoy the benefits of salvation and the pleasures of sin at the same time are tempting Christ.

It kept Israel from Canaan. It's keeping men from their Canaan today.

Murmuring: Complaining, criticizing, faultfinding, slandering, rumoring—all these and more are classified as murmuring.

"How great a forest a little fire kindles!" (James 3:5 NKJV).

The tongue is like that. Small remarks, cutting comments, and sarcastic jibes eventually create roaring bonfires of hate, warfare, and enmity. Consuming relationships, it leaves nothing but embers.

Men murmur against their company. They murmur against the preacher. They murmur against God's Word. Then they complain when they don't see God's blessing in their lives.

No Canaan there.

God wants us to be free of the big five sins. He calls us to enter into our Canaan land—the place of rest, blessing, success, ability, and authority.

It is the place where he desires you to live.

THE CHALLENGE

+ Every man is given the opportunity to enter his Canaan, to develop his potential of manhood to the maximum.

+ The five sins are still the five root causes for men living in unfulfilled potential. They are basic to all humanity.

+ Lust goes beyond the sexual. Lust can show itself in a variety of forms: covetousness, gluttony, drunkenness, power hunger, and unbridled ambition. *But lust in any form knows no peace.* Peace can come only through the Prince of Peace, the Lord Jesus Christ, through the power of his Spirit.

+ Murmuring in its simplest form is nothing more or less than negative confession.

THE WORD

Put on the Lord Jesus Christ, and make no provision for the flesh, to fulfill its lusts.   Romans 13:14 NKJV

A greedy person is really an idol worshiper—he loves and worships the good things of this life more than God.   Ephesians 5:5 TLB

You shall not tempt the LORD your God.
                                    Deuteronomy 6:16 NKJV

And the people murmured against Moses, saying, What shall we drink?   Exodus 15:24 KJV

16

YOU DON'T OWN ANYTHING

Men don't own anything. We are only stewards.

God made man to be a leader and a steward.

Men don't own anything—we are only stewards.

Health, marriage, children, lands, businesses, a wife's love—over all these, we are only stewards. Everything belongs to God—he gave it all to us. It is what we do with it, how we take care of it, for which we must give an account.

Stewardship is what God gave Adam to do, and he has never rescinded it. Given the responsibility of stewardship over the earth, Adam derived his greatest satisfaction from the reproduction process that God had established for the replenishing of the earth.

From then until now, a man's source of fulfillment has never changed. Man still derives his greatest satisfaction from the reproductive process of his stewardship over the earth. Whether farming, running a lathe, or exercising authority as the chief executive officer of a corporation—a man's job is still a man's basic satisfaction in life.

The workplace is where a man's unique desire is basically satisfied. The farmer's satisfaction with the reproductive process is found at harvest time. A salesman finds it when the customer buys the product or service, an architect when his plans become a finished building, an accountant when his audit is completed, and a preacher when his altar call produces results. We men were created that way. It's never changed.

The three basic responsibilities of any steward are to guide, guard, and govern.

Every man has these three functions in the home and community. In practical terms, this means to direct, protect, and correct. In relationships such as parenting, it is to nourish, cherish, and admonish. Fathers who are godly stewards are the earth's—and the family's—greatest blessing.

Men make the mistake of thinking they are possessors. That thinking causes us to act independently of God. And that is where all our problems begin. Adam acted independently of God. And look where it got him.

For men and even ministers, our work or ministry can become an idol. We become so devoted to it that we do not take time to worship God, wait in his presence, or spend time ministering to him.

Many men will trade wives and keep businesses. But God's divine pattern is to cause a man to change and enable him as a husband to minister to his wife. This was God's intention ever since Eve was first called Adam's "helpmate." God holds the man responsible for becoming a minister to his wife.

The great complaint among wives, is, "My husband can connect with the whole world, but he can't minister to me."

We defend ourselves on the basis of busyness, fatigue, workload, economic pressure, client anxiety—ministering to the whole world. Admittedly, it is taxing.

I have seen this syndrome at work in countless lives: couples fall in love and marry, but as business grows, children come, church needs demand attention—more and more, they do things through the kids, for the church, or on business.

Men don't possess a wife's love. We are only stewards of it. Our wife's love is God's gift to us.

What you need to realize is that you fell in love with your wife, and after everything else is gone, you still have each other. Or you will, if you have been a good steward of the marriage.

Take her away and give her your undivided attention. Fall in love again periodically.

Steward your money, steward your job, steward your family's love and respect. Be a good steward of all God gives you.

THE CHALLENGE

+ Men must be good stewards of our wives, children, careers, homes, and finances, for we will give account of our stewardship. God the Creator holds us accountable for what he has given us.

+ Men possess a mind but don't own it. We are only stewards of it. If we do not exercise good stewardship of our minds, they will lose capabilities.

+ Too many men take their wife's love for granted and fail to realize it is a free gift.

+ Poor stewardship of a wife's love can cause it to fail, falter, wither, and die. Good stewardship can make it bloom, flower, and produce the loveliest, most beautiful relationship on earth.

THE WORD

Then the LORD God took the man and put him in the garden of Eden to tend and keep it.

Genesis 2:15 NKJV

Each of you should use whatever gift you have received to serve others, as faithful stewards of God's grace in its various forms. 1 Peter 4:10

Moreover it is required in stewards, that a man be found faithful. 1 Corinthians 4:2 KJV

17

THE PLAYBOY PROBLEM

Sin promises to serve and please but only desires
to deceive and dominate.

On the East Coast, I had just concluded a brief Bible study when a young woman drew me to one side for prayer.

"I have a problem," she said, her face tight and tears welling.

"What is it?" I asked.

"I don't really know," she stammered, "but my husband says I have a problem."

"What does your husband say your problem is?" I asked.

"My husband says he needs to look at porn before he can have sex with me," she blurted between sobs. "He says if I really loved him, I would understand why, that it's my problem."

"What does your husband do for a living?" I inquired.

"He's a youth minister."

Astonished, I said, "Your husband may be a minister, but he is also a pornographer."

Her head snapped to attention. She never expected to hear her husband described as a pornographer. And yet, his lifestyle made him exactly that.

Pornography—a plague in society in every nation under the sun—is idolatry. With it, a man creates images in the mind to which the act of habitual masturbation is an act of worship to that idol or image. Pornography, like all manner of sinfulness, promises to serve and please but only deceives and dominates. While promising intimacy, it only produces addiction and emptiness.

Satan comes to steal, kill, and destroy. But he never shows himself as a messenger of evil. He always appears as an "angel of light," making temptations appear normal and desirable. Satan has made pornography seem harmless and mainstream, as if "everybody's doing it," so it must be okay.

Pornography perpetuates puberty. The pornography industry unashamedly targets twelve- to seventeen-year-old men. It's an obvious trap, yet men fall into it every day. Ironically, one way to remain an adolescent is to do what our culture marks as "adult."

Such deception is sent to destroy men, marriages, women, and children. Perhaps a cultural lifestyle views perversion and pornography as acceptable. But God views it as sin. Sin brings bondage.

When pornography is in the mind, a husband can easily reduce his wife to become a source for fulfilling his fantasy. The problem is, in real life, wives don't come airbrushed to perfection. Husbands who love their wives only for sex make themselves users and predators and her a victim or his prey. The husband no longer values her except physically, and the marriage disintegrates.

The thought is parent to the deed. Any man can be led astray by his own lusts. "Then, after desire has conceived, it gives birth to sin; and sin, when it is full-grown, gives birth to death" (James 1:15).

More than one kind of death exists. Financial death is bankruptcy. Marital death is divorce.

In the sex-charged atmosphere of our culture, keeping ourselves pure from sexual images and immorality requires constant vigilance.

Internet filters are a must, but nothing is as powerful for real help as the Word of God and the Holy Spirit. No matter what the temptation, God's covenant-keeping power is sufficient for any need.

You don't escape *from* temptation but *to* God. Filling our minds with the Word of God, filling our thoughts with prayer, and filling our time with accountability and training— these are remedies against the negative pulls from the culture around us.

Tackle sin like a man. Ask for help.

Confess and forsake pornography.

THE CHALLENGE

+ Sin promises to serve and please but only desires to deceive and dominate.

+ Pornography promises intimacy but only produces addiction and emptiness.

+ Husbands who love their wives only for sex make themselves users and predators and her a victim or prey.

+ Pornography perpetuates puberty.

+ It is not enough to be delivered *from* sin; it is enough to be delivered *to* righteousness.

THE WORD

Whoever conceals their sins does not prosper, but the one who confesses and renounces them finds mercy.
Proverbs 28:13

Very truly I tell you, everyone who sins is a slave to sin. John 8:34

After desire has conceived, it gives birth to sin; and sin, when it is full-grown, gives birth to death.
James 1:15

Marriage should be honored by all, and the marriage bed kept pure, for God will judge the adulterer and all the sexually immoral. Hebrews 13:4

18

PRAYER PRODUCES INTIMACY

You become intimate with the one to whom you pray, for whom you pray, and with whom you pray.

One day the phone rang in my office. A female caller wanted to know if I was the Dr. Cole who had seminars for men. When she was assured that I was, she began, "I have listened to your audios, and I think they are powerful in speaking to men. I want you to tell men how we women really feel."

She had my attention.

"My husband is a good man. He never misses church. We are both Christians and love the Lord.

"But in all the years we have been married," the woman said, "my husband has never talked to me about God. We talk about everything else. It was fifteen years after our wedding before he ever prayed in front of me—and then it was only because I was sick, and I asked him to.

"Please tell the men wherever you go that we women want them to be leaders in prayer and Bible study. If he would just be a leader, I could love him even more."

Prayer produces intimacy.

You become intimate with the one *to whom* you pray, the one *for whom* you pray, and the one *with whom* you pray.

Moses went up to Mount Sinai—the place of prayer—and stayed so long that finally God was able to speak to him as "friend to friend." Why?

Because prayer produces intimacy.

Jesus had become so intimate with the Father in prayer that on the Mount of Transfiguration, the glory of the Father's presence shone through him.

When a man prays with his wife, he becomes intimate with her. In true spiritual prayer, the intimacy developed is far greater than a physical union. It is in spirit.

Some years back, the morning sessions of the Pennsylvania conference where I was speaking were over, and I was returning to my room to pack. A man approached and asked if he could tell me his story. I listened. I'm glad I did.

The man said the principle that prayer produces intimacy had really impressed him, and he desired to put that into practice in his marriage.

At night, there never seemed to be a time or place for prayer. Finally, he and his wife agreed that after the children had gone to bed, they would go to their bedroom and read a psalm and pray together.

During their seven years of marriage, they had had continuous problems concerning their sex life. But after three months of reading the Word of God and praying together, they noticed that without even realizing it, their problems had been resolved. He told me, "When you said prayer produces intimacy, you weren't kidding."

As they prayed together, they began to communicate spirit to spirit. They discovered a new ability to talk about things they had never been able to discuss before. The result of both was intimacy in marriage.

As you read this, if you have not prayed for your wife, stop right now and ask God to forgive you. Begin a change this very moment. Don't even read another word until you have prayed for her.

Pray *for* her and *with* her. Develop your intimacy.

To have a deeply intimate marriage in body and spirit, the marriage God intends for all men, you don't have any options.

THE CHALLENGE

+ Sexual relations are one thing; spiritual union is another. If you really want to be one with your wife, then pray for her and with her.

+ The failure of a man to pray for his wife means that he can have a physical intimacy, but he does not develop the intimacy of spirit that produces true oneness.

+ Men who know their wives in prayer also know them in the living room, the kitchen, and the bedroom.

+ Distance can be measured by miles or affection. Prayer knows no distance.

THE WORD

The earnest prayer of a righteous man has great power and wonderful results. James 5:16 TLB

Men always ought to pray and not lose heart. Luke 18:1 NKJV

Again, truly I tell you that if two of you on earth agree about anything they ask for, it will be done for them by my Father in heaven. Matthew 18:19

For where two or three gather in my name, there am I with them. Matthew 18:20

19

SCRIPTURAL ILLITERACY

**God's Word is the sole source of our faith and
the absolute rule of our conduct.**

To grow in Christ, we must be literate in the Word of God.

Too many men who name the name of Christ attempt to live a Christian life based on what people say—advice given, articles read, audios and videos—instead of relying on the Word of God.

When the tough times come, a man will realize that trying to build a solid foundation of faith on such underpinnings is like attempting to build the Empire State Building on the ocean.

Building a godly life on the sand of scriptural illiteracy is impossible.

Jesus gave us the wisdom of God in the parable about building on a rock or on sand. "Therefore everyone who hears these words of mine and puts them into practice is like a wise man who built his house on the rock....But everyone who hears these words of mine and does not put them into practice is like a foolish man who built his house on sand" (Matthew 7:24, 26).

Building on sand may seem safe—until the storm comes. There will be nothing to stand on when tough times come. The Word of God is the solid foundation for building your life.

God speaks to us from his Word—the Bible. That is the rule, not the exception, so daily reading of the Word is vital.

Knowledge of God's Word is a bulwark against deception, temptation, accusation, and even persecution. You must be scripturally literate to those desiring to overcome the world, the flesh, and the devil. The Bible is not merely a good source for playing trivia games. The Bible is the very foundation upon which both natural and eternal life rests.

The Holy Spirit inscribes God's Word on our hearts as we *study* and *meditate on* the Word.

First, the Bible tells us to *study* the Word of God (2 Timothy 2:15).

The study of God's Word is like mining for precious minerals and jewels. It takes effort. The book of Proverbs states we will discover understanding in God's Word when we search for it as for buried treasure (Proverbs 2:3–4). In contrast, little effort is required to obtain good advice, listen to a sermon, or watch television.

We are to love God with *all* of our minds. In tough days, if we do not diligently apply ourselves to study, we will not survive the whims of doctrine that float past us. We cannot base our lives on God's Word mixed with lies from a decadent society.

Second, we must *meditate on* the Word—that means to pause and think about it. "I will meditate on Your precepts, and contemplate Your ways" (Psalm 119:15 NKJV).

And, third, we must *obey* it. "Do not merely listen to the word, and so deceive yourselves. Do what it says" (James 1:22).

The only Scripture you believe is the one you obey.

There is a difference between reading the Bible and living it. As much difference as there is between heaven and hell.

Giving lip service to God is hypocritical and causes instability in a man's ways. In the tensions of life—wrestling between choices of family and profession, recreation and work, ethics and cheating, church and pleasure—when the choice is made to obey God's Word, the result is peace. It is harmony with God, self, and others.

God's Word is the sole source of our faith and the absolute rule of our conduct. God's promise assures us that meditating on the Word and doing what it says will bring success.

Study God's Word. Act on it in faith.

It is your solid foundation.

THE CHALLENGE

+ The more Word you have in you, the more Christlike you become. The less Word you have in you, the less Christlike you become. It's an elementary formula, but it separates the men from the boys.

+ The man who seeks the daily application of Bible study and prayer, and hungers and thirsts for God, wants to be part of what God is doing on earth in this hour.

+ The man who has been a believer for many years and never gone beyond memorization of John 3:16 is just as immature as the man who received Christ yesterday.

+ Submission to the Word brings resistance to the devil and power over the flesh.

THE WORD

For the word of God is alive and active. Sharper than any double-edged sword, it penetrates even to dividing soul and spirit, joints and marrow; it judges the thoughts and attitudes of the heart.   Hebrews 4:12

Submit yourselves therefore to God. Resist the devil, and he will flee from you.   James 4:7 KJV

Study to [show yourself] approved unto God, a workman that [need] not to be ashamed, rightly dividing the word of truth.   2 Timothy 2:15 KJV

20

THE 30-DAY EXPERIMENT

The one who listens before he talks will succeed.

One of the most successful insurance men on the West Coast stood up to address a sales convention. He had sold more insurance than anyone in the room. The air was keen with anticipation to hear his secrets.

He began slowly, relaxing against the corner of the podium.

"I know everyone has talked about how much insurance I've sold," he said. "But when I started in this business a few years ago, a successful friend gave me some advice. All I've ever done is just follow that advice."

Everyone leaned forward, waiting.

"My friend told me, 'You can get a man to do anything you want him to if you only listen to him long enough.'

"When I go and talk to someone, I listen to them. After I've listened to them long enough, I simply say, 'Okay, why don't you just sign right here?' And they do it.

"When you've asked them enough questions and listened to them long enough, it's your turn to speak. All you do is ask for their signature." With that, he sat down.

Some men are talkers. Others are listeners. The one who listens before he talks will succeed. Listen until you hear the need, then simply meet the need.

Listening is not a random function of your body. Listening is ministry. God's Word repeatedly says, "He who has ears to hear, let him hear."

At the end of a morning meeting in Phoenix, Arizona, a couple approached me.

"Our thirteen-year-old daughter has run away from home," the wife said. "Please pray that God will bring her back."

We prayed. When they returned a few hours later for the evening meeting, their daughter was with them. She wouldn't talk to her parents, but she agreed to talk with me.

When I asked how things were with her mother, she said, "Fine."

"How about Dad?" I asked.

She became sullen.

"He never listens to me," she finally said. "He blames me for everything."

I got it. When we rejoined her parents, I offered that father the biggest challenge of his life.

"I'll pray with you for your daughter under one condition." Looking directly at him, I said, "You're going to be responsible for the change in your daughter. Can you accept that responsibility?"

He nodded.

"Here's the condition. For the next thirty days, your daughter can say anything to you she wants to say, any time she wants to say it. You can only listen. You can't answer until those thirty days are up."

The father was stunned. After a long silence, he agreed.

Three months later, I was back in Phoenix and saw them again. They were a different family—outgoing, happy, standing close to one another.

"It was hard at first," the father said, "but I wanted a change. So, I listened to my daughter, and then I listened some more. That's when I realized that some of what she said was right. I was wrong.

"When I asked her to forgive me, she began to change. Our whole family is different today. My problem? I was so busy, I didn't take time to listen to my daughter."

The unusual experiment proved the point: *men must learn to listen.*

As the leader, steward, minister, counselor—you must have the courage to be the man your family needs you to be.

Listen to your family's needs. If needed, conduct your own 30-Day Experiment.

THE CHALLENGE

+ Men are so occupied with their "busyness" that they leave the ministry of "listening to the children" in their wives' hands. That is an abdication of part of your manhood. *Listen.*

+ As men, we must study our wives and our children—and do it in the light of God's Word.

+ Men need to listen to their wives and children to affirm their uniqueness, learn their needs, and make the relationship grow.

+ Commit to spend time one-on-one weekly or monthly with every member of your family just to *listen.*

THE WORD

My dear brothers and sisters, take note of this: Everyone should be quick to listen, slow to speak and slow to become angry.   James 1:19

And you, fathers, do not provoke your children to wrath, but bring them up in the training and admonition of the Lord.   Ephesians 6:4 NKJV

The way of a fool is right in his own eyes, but a wise man listens to advice.   Proverbs 12:15 ESV

21

FIVE PROPOSITIONS CONCERNING GOD'S WORD

We trust God because we trust his Word.

A major sign of manhood is in a man's word. To be conformed to the image of Christ, our words must conform to God's Word. God's Word is trustworthy.

Here are five propositions concerning God's Word.

1. *God's Word is his bond.*

When God gives us his Word, we can trust him. He gives himself as the bond that his Word is truth. "For when God made a promise to Abraham, because He could swear by no one greater, He swore by Himself" (Hebrews 6:13 NKJV). God can swear by no one greater than himself.

In the new covenant, Christ himself is the Word that confirms the promise of salvation.

2. *God's Word is the expression of his nature.*

Jesus Christ came to earth as the express image of the person of God (Hebrews 1:3). He told Philip, "Anyone who has seen me has seen the Father" (John 14:9). John teaches us, "In the beginning was the Word, and the Word was with God, and the Word was God" (John 1:1).

Christ is the living Word of God. The very nature of God is revealed in Jesus Christ. As Jesus is God's Word revealed, so the Bible is God's Word revealed to us. The Word is made alive in our hearts by the Holy Spirit.

3. *God's Word is the measure of his character.*

When Jesus Christ referred to himself as the Alpha and Omega, he was using the first and last letters of the Greek alphabet (Revelation 1:8). Meaning, he is the beginning and the end, the first and last. This is a divine way of revealing the large measure of God's character to us.

There is no end to God's character, therefore, no end to his Word. No matter how much of himself he reveals, even in eternity, there will be no end to the revelation of his character. The measure of God's character is in his Word.

4. *God's Word is magnified above his name.*

God's name is as good as his Word. If his Word is no good, his name is no good.

The Word tells us that "faith comes by hearing, and hearing by the word of God" (Romans 10:17 NKJV).

Our faith grows by reading and meditating on God's Word. Our prayer of faith is always made on the basis of his Word. When Jesus said to use his name, he was literally telling us to use his authority (John 14:13). The use of his name comes from the authority and trustworthiness of his Word.

5. *God's Word is the sole source of faith and the absolute rule of conduct.*

God's Word alone, accepted by faith, has the power of salvation. We are saved by the incorruptible seed of the Word of God.

Neither time, nor chance, nor elements, nor men can invalidate, nullify, neutralize, cancel, or make void the wisdom or power of God's Word.

God's Word stands tough and trustworthy. Immerse yourself in it. Learn to trust God and his Word. Commit to reading the Word daily.

THE CHALLENGE

+ In this present age, we must awaken ourselves to the urgent need to study, restore our love for truth, and renew our reverence for God's Word.

+ The truths of God's Word and the absence of truth in the world today both have tremendous relevance to the way we live our lives.

+ When men find God's pattern for their lives and base their faith on the principles in his Word, they become successful in all they do.

+ God's Word is the sole source of our faith and the absolute rule of our conduct.

THE WORD

The Son is the radiance of God's glory and the exact representation of his being, sustaining all things by his powerful word.   Hebrews 1:3

So shall my word be that goeth forth out of my mouth: it shall not return unto me void, but it shall accomplish that which I please, and it shall prosper in the thing whereto I sent it.   Isaiah 55:11 KJV

Let your heart retain my words; keep my commands, and live.   Proverbs 4:4 NKJV

Jesus answered him, saying, "It is written, 'Man shall not live by bread alone, but by every word of God.'"
                                        Luke 4:4 NKJV

22

FIVE PROPOSITIONS CONCERNING A MAN'S WORD

You believe the message because you believe the man.

Because we are created in the image of God, whatever God's Word is to him, our word is to be to us. The same truths relative to God's Word apply to our word. God watches over his Word to perform it (Jeremiah 1:12). So also, we should watch over our word to perform it.

Here are five propositions concerning our word that mirror the five propositions concerning God's Word.

1. *Our word is our bond.*

In my youth, the character of men was much stronger and richer in integrity than it is now. When a man gave you his word and shook your hand as the seal, it was better than a signed contract.

Today, lawyers draw up legal papers with infinite pains to cover every detail of the agreement. And still, the paper is only as good as the character of the people who sign it. Where men do not hold to a high value of truth, they do not place a high value on their word.

A man's word is his bond.

2. Our word is the expression of our nature.

In the early days of my Christian experience, we were taught to "sanctify our speech." "Gosh" and "darn" were considered euphemisms for "God" and "damn." We conscientiously removed these "minced oaths" from our vocabularies.

Salvation was to us a total experience. Inside and out, the Holy Spirit was at work to cleanse us from *all* unrighteousness—including our words.

Strange that, today, the world uses Christ's name to swear, while Christians swear by his name. Peddlers of profanity will be held responsible for making the use of the vilest profanity an everyday occurrence. The idea of purging our language needs to be revived.

Men's words reveal their nature within. That is why Jesus said, "For out of the abundance of the heart [the] mouth speaks" (Luke 6:45).

Our words reflect our manhood in Christ.

3. Our word is the measure of our character.

The honesty of a man's heart, the depth of manly character, is shown by how he keeps his word. It's called integrity.

The prophet Job cried out in his deepest need, "I will not remove [my] integrity from me" (Job 27:5 KJV).

4. *Our word is magnified above our name.*

Our name is only as good as our word. If our word is no good, our name is no good.

Men who do not value their word diminish their personal worth. An amazing number of people submit false résumés for professional positions. Men exaggerate and lie. When they are discovered, they fight against being exposed or fired. Regardless of the level of their work, their value drops when they are deemed untrustworthy. Not valuing your word diminishes your name.

5. *Our word is the source of faith and rule of conduct for those to whom we give it.*

What a man is like is shown by how he keeps his word. It is the one true measure of his integrity.

A man's integrity is revealed in his words and backed by his conduct in his home, job, church, and community.

A man is more than his message.

You believe in the message because you believe in the man.

THE CHALLENGE

+ A man's word is the expression of his nature.

+ A man's nature, his character, makes his word believable.

+ Every word has creative power. That's why Scripture says life and death are in the power of the tongue. Change your words, change your life.

+ A man who uses the name of Jesus as an epithet in everyday conversation cannot be truthful on Sunday in worshipping that same name.

THE WORD

The LORD detests lying lips, but he delights in people who are trustworthy.   Proverbs 12:22

When words are many, transgression is not lacking, but whoever restrains his lips is prudent.
                Proverbs 10:19 ESV

By your words you will be acquitted, and by your words you will be condemned.   Matthew 12:37

Let your "Yes" be "Yes," and your "No," "No." For whatever is more than these is from the evil one.
                Matthew 5:37 NKJV

23

THE POVERTY SYNDROME

Prosperity is the natural, sequentially ordered result of righteousness in life.

"**B**lessed is the man whose delight is in the Word of the Lord. He is like a tree planted by streams of water—whatever he does prospers." That's my paraphrase of Psalm 1:1–3. To paraphrase further: *Prosperity is the natural, sequentially ordered result of righteousness in life.*

Righteousness means "right standing with God." Wherever there is righteousness, there is prosperity—in mission, in marriage, and also in money.

Financial poverty is an enemy. It is a blessing only to those who embrace it, a curse to those who don't. "Being poor" and "living in poverty" are not necessarily the same. A "poverty syndrome" afflicts the poor and the rich alike. I've seen men from all walks of life living in poverty and needing to confront the poverty syndrome.

My friend Ralph, a painting contractor, received the largest contract he had ever been offered. He knew if he signed the contract, it would mean hiring new help and buying new equipment.

He struggled to decide what to do until he read God's Word one morning: "To him who knows to do good and does not do it, to him it is sin" (James 4:17 NKJV). He realized God was speaking to him, giving him an opportunity to expand his business. Not to do it would be sinning against God.

To refuse God's favor is to deny his prosperity.

Ralph fought the "poverty syndrome." It took everything he had to accept the contract. He did, and moved to a new level of prosperity—financially, and in faith and dependence on God.

A man's rejection of God's desire to increase his life through Jesus Christ is unfair—to his family, his church, his community, and God's grace.

Men who fail to prosper through a sense of unworthiness do not understand that if they are in Christ, and Christ is in them, their identity with Christ makes them worthy.

My family and I learned this the hard way. Needing a new vehicle, I sensed God direct me to a comfortable car. I decided against it. I didn't consider myself worthy of God's goodness.

The small economy car I bought instead became a "curse" to our family. It broke constantly, it was in the shop more than on the road, every member of the family had a wreck in it, and the engine, transmission, and most of the body were replaced. After three years, I was sitting in a coffee shop one morning when I saw a man who worked at the dealership.

"Do you still own that lemon?" he called out.

We laughed. I told him it was parked right out front. He asked if I'd be willing to sell it to use as a "loaner." I walked over to his table, handed him the keys, told him to mail me a check with the transfer of ownership, and called my daughter to come pick me up. *I was free!*

My family had been victimized by my own "poverty syndrome." I had confused "humility" with disobedience.

It is not wrong to be rich, but it is wrong to trust in riches, to think you have the power to get them apart from God's favor, to use them only for self, to lust after them, to seek them through "get-rich-quick" schemes, to desire them immorally, or to obtain or use them illegally.

Riches are not wrong. It is what they do to us that is wrong.

Riches with righteousness can be a blessing.

When God calls us to prosper, it is our responsibility to obey.

THE CHALLENGE

+ Jesus Christ is worthy of everything in heaven and on earth. Identification with him gives worthiness to a man's life.

+ Everything we have from God is by faith in Christ and in his worthiness. Jesus makes worthy the worst of us.

+ The deceitfulness of riches comes when you think you have enough, but it never is, and there is no contentment. Contentment is necessary because it eliminates monetary deception.

THE WORD

Blessed is the one who does not walk in step with the wicked or stand in the way that sinners take or sit in the company of mockers, but whose delight is in the law of the LORD, and who meditates on his law day and night. That person is like a tree planted by streams of water, which yields its fruit in season and whose leaf does not wither—whatever they do prospers. Psalm 1:1–3

Godliness actually is a source of great gain when accompanied by contentment [that contentment which comes from a sense of inner confidence based on the sufficiency of God]. 1 Timothy 6:6 AMP

The LORD will command the blessing on you in your barns and in all that you undertake. And he will bless you in the land that the LORD your God is giving you.   Deuteronomy 28:8 ESV

Now he who supplies seed to the sower and bread for food will also supply and increase your store of seed and will enlarge the harvest of your righteousness.

           2 Corinthians 9:10

24

THE GREAT RIP-OFF

Men unwittingly teach their families not to trust them.

God is a maximizer of men. Satan is a usurper.

Christ is truth. Satan is "the father of lies" (John 8:44).

Since the garden of Eden, Satan has attacked God's Word to lure men into sin. Satan not only tries to "rip off" God's Word. He tries to steal our word, as well.

Think of a father who promises to take his son fishing. The son immediately prepares—putting the tackle box and fishing pole under his bed, dreaming of the day. The night before their fishing trip, the father's friend calls with tickets to a football game. The father accepts the offer.

Early the next morning, the son is up, eager to get going, only to be told his dad is going to the game instead. Disappointed, the son sulks. Days of resentful attitude follow until, in exasperation, the father tells the son to change or be punished. The boy's disappointment turns to resentment, then deepens into rebellion.

Without realizing his own culpability and responsibility, the father helplessly watches the hardening of his son's heart.

I've listened to men who give God their word and even then fail to keep it. They do not realize their word is being "ripped off." Their enemy of their own shallow character, coupled with Satan's conspiracy to steal words, kills a man's influence and destroys his relationships.

What about the man who constantly promises his wife that he will change, or buy her something, or take her places, or fix something, but never does? Little does he realize that he is teaching her to mistrust his word. A wife who no longer believes her husband's word is unable to believe in him.

One Saturday morning, I was talking with people after speaking at a conference when a man stopped me. He locked his eyes on me and said, "In all my life, I've never had a man talk to me the way you just did."

"I apologize if I was too hard—" I began.

"Not that!" he interrupted. "You told me what was wrong with my life. I am a pastor. Today my wife won't go to church with me, my children have turned their backs on God, and my congregation is smaller than ever. I have been blaming everyone else, but it's my fault."

"Well—" I started.

He cut me off again.

"I heard the truth," he said, "that my word is my bond, the source of faith to people who listen to me, and my name is only as good as my word. For the first time in my life, I know what I did.

"All my life, I made promises of what I would do for my family, knowing even as I said it, I probably couldn't do it. I gave myself credit for the promises. I realize now that, to my family, I was a liar.

"Before today, I considered myself to be a man of God's Word. Now, I know I am not a man of my word. If I were a man of God's Word, I would be a man of my word.

"You have just unraveled my whole life. Now, I'm going to go home and try, with God's help, to put it all back together."

Tough? Yeah, that's tough. But real? You bet.

Be a man of God's Word. Be a man of your word.

THE CHALLENGE

- Keep your word to your family. To a child, a broken promise is really a lie.

- Trust is extended to the limit of truth and no more.

- Satan's attacks on men's lives today still start with God's Word.

- A leader who lies to his people will find they will not follow him, because he is unbelievable.

THE WORD

The tongue has the power of life and death, and those who love it will eat its fruit. Proverbs 18:21

For by your words you will be justified, and by your words you will be condemned.
Matthew 12:37 NKJV

You have been trapped by what you said, ensnared by the words of your mouth. Proverbs 6:2

25

BORN-AGAIN MARRIAGE

Marriage can be the closest thing to heaven or hell on this earth.

Betty and Bill met at church youth meetings and were married while still in their teens. Bill became a successful businessman. Betty became an extremely popular, active wife and mother. They were the model family in the affairs of business, community, and church.

But fifteen years into the marriage, Bill and Betty were locked in a cold war. Tension between them was running high.

During that time, they heard me teaching on the principle that true manhood is Christlikeness. These words imprinted themselves upon Bill's mind, and he meditated on them.

Inevitably, another crisis occurred at home. After a long, heated exchange, Bill burst out of the house and headed for the car.

Once inside the car, he put his head down on the steering wheel and clenched his fists. He was almost nauseous from the fighting, bickering, barbs, and fiery exchanges.

He knew it was wrong.

He needed help.

Pounding his fists on the steering wheel, he began to shout, "God, you've got to do something! I can't go on any longer!"

He rarely shed a tear, but Bill began to cry compulsively. His sobs turned to sighs of helplessness. "Jesus, you're my Savior. Help me."

Minutes passed. He composed himself, started the car, and drove away. As he drove, Bill thought about those characteristics of Christlikeness I had shared. He began to see that the marks of Christlikeness were missing in his marriage.

He and Betty as individuals knew those qualities in their lives. But they were not in their marriage.

With a start, something occurred to him.

He and Betty had both been born again—and their marriage needed the same experience. Their marriage needed to be born again.

He turned the car around and raced home.

"I need to talk to you," he said to Betty as he led her upstairs to their bedroom. "Do you remember when Jesus came into your life?"

"Of course," she said. "It was wonderful."

"When we married," he said, "we had a wedding. But that was it. We've never had family devotions. We've never prayed together. We've never read the Word together. Our boys have never seen us talk to God except over meals."

Bill looked at her intently. "Our marriage needs to be born again."

They sat on the bed and talked, sharing their most intimate feelings and thoughts.

Bill opened himself up to her for the first time in over a decade, exposing his heart, asking her forgiveness for his many wrongs.

Betty shared with him her longings, desires, and hurts. Together, they climbed over the walls of defensiveness they had built to protect themselves from vulnerability. They gave and received forgiveness.

In the early hours of the morning, they knelt and called on Jesus to make their marriage new.

It was the start of a new kind of life.

The next night, as they headed to their seats to enjoy a ball game at Angels Stadium, they clung like lovers who had just discovered each other.

He turned to her as they climbed the steps and said, "Do you know, I think this is the greatest day of my life! I feel absolutely free." They both laughed.

A born-again marriage.

Bill had a good idea. Maybe it would be good for you, too.

THE CHALLENGE

+ If you need a born-again marriage, pray for wisdom to win back your wife's love.

+ Doing your first works over and regaining your first love is the only sure way to renew your relationships, both with God and with your wife.

+ When a husband is loving his wife, not just lusting after her, he desires to satisfy her at the expense of himself.

+ Renewed revelation, understanding, and appreciation are the best ways to keep a marriage relationship fresh and real.

THE WORD

Two are better than one, because they have a good return for their labor: If either of them falls down, one can help the other up.   Ecclesiastes 4:9–10

He who finds a wife finds what is good and receives favor from the LORD.   Proverbs 18:22

"Haven't you read," he replied, "that at the beginning the Creator 'made them male and female,' and said, 'For this reason a man will leave his father and mother and be united to his wife, and the two will become one flesh'? So they are no longer two, but one flesh. Therefore what God has joined together, let no one separate."   Matthew 19:4–6

26

RELEASE FOR YOUR LIFE

Men need to know how to forgive.

Men need to know how to forgive. Many men think that forgiveness is a sign of weakness. Nothing could be further from the truth.

I was teaching in Cleveland when a man approached and asked me to pray with him for the salvation of his two sons. As we started to pray, he said, "They are both alcoholics, and I know that if the Lord saves them, they will be freed from alcohol. Their families won't be hurt anymore."

I bowed my head to pray with him, then stopped, looked at him, and asked him to look at me. He still had his head bowed.

There was some noise around us, so I repeated myself to get his attention. His head snapped up.

"Were you ever an alcoholic?" I asked him. He hesitated to answer. He had been a believer for many years, and that was all in the past. He didn't want to have that brought up to him again.

But I pressed the point.

"Have you ever been an alcoholic?" I asked again.

"Yes," he answered softly.

"Were your children at home at the time?"

"Yes."

"Have you ever gone to your children and asked them to forgive you for being an alcoholic when they were at home?"

"Oh, I'm sure they have," the man replied.

"That's not the issue," I said. "Have you ever gone to your sons and deliberately sat down with them and said to them, 'Forgive me for being an alcoholic and acting like I did when you were at home'?"

The man looked down. "No."

"Then I'll pray with you," I stated, "and I'll believe God with you for the salvation of your sons—under one condition."

"What's that?" he wondered.

"That you will go to your sons and ask them to forgive you of your alcoholism," I said. I looked intently at him, waiting for his answer.

He returned my gaze, then agreed. We prayed.

That man's sons hated his alcoholism. They never forgave him for it. In John 20:23 (NKJV), we read, "If you forgive the sins of any, they are forgiven them [released]; if you retain the sins of any [don't forgive them], they are retained." By forgiving someone, we release that person and their sin. When we do not forgive them, we hold on to those sins.

Because the man's sons never forgave him, they held onto their father's sin and became like the thing they hated. Unforgiveness, bitterness, and hate binds sin to people. Forgiveness releases it. They had bound themselves to their father's sin.

Many fathers believe it is weak to admit they have failed their children and to ask their forgiveness. That is not true. Leading children into forgiveness provides a true release, a break from the past—both for parent and child.

Forgiving our own parents is a true release for us. It can also be a break for our parents.

In forgiving someone's sins, we release them. When we do not forgive them, those sins are retained. Forgiveness is essential to remove sin.

This is a kingdom principle and the basis for our Christian faith. When we ask God to forgive us, and he does, he releases us from our sins forever. He will never remember those sins against us again.

What joy God's forgiveness brings. A release of God's Spirit. Relief for the mind. Power in the life.

To be maximized in your manhood, learn to forgive and to ask for forgiveness. It is Christlike both to give and receive forgiveness.

THE CHALLENGE

+ Forgiveness opens; unforgiveness closes.

+ To know true manhood, accept responsibility for your sins and ask forgiveness.

+ What you forgive, you release. What you do not forgive, you retain.

+ Sins are not inherited. However, through unforgiveness, sins pass from father to son and daughter, from generation to generation.

THE WORD

Jesus said… "If you forgive the sins of any, they are forgiven them; if you retain the sins of any, they are retained."   John 20:22-23 NKJV

And when you stand praying, if you hold anything against anyone, forgive them, so that your Father in heaven may forgive you your sins.   Mark 11:25

For if you forgive other people when they sin against you, your heavenly Father will also forgive you.
Matthew 6:14

27

THE HOLE IN THE DOOR

Forgiveness is always in spirit, not just in word.

My son Paul had a new driver's license in his wallet.

I came home for a day or two in the middle of ministerial travels, and Paul asked me that question that all dads "love" to hear: "Can I have the car?"

"Why?" I asked.

"I want to go to youth camp at Mt. Lassen."

I had a mental file drawer full of reasons why he shouldn't take it.

"That's a brand new car."

"I know it."

"You've only had your driver's license a few weeks."

"I know it."

"Youth camp is four hundred miles away."

"I know it."

"What makes you think you can have the car?" I finally asked.

"Well, I want to go to youth camp," Paul responded simply.

"You're not taking that new car four hundred miles to youth camp," I said.

"Oh, I forgot. I need the credit card, too."

"I'm not going to give you the car," I countered.

"I've been driving for a year with a permit," he reasoned, correctly.

"Just don't even ask me," I retorted. "I said no, and that's it. I don't want to hear it again."

Case closed.

Paul turned and kicked at the floor, flushed with anger and disappointment. He walked down the hall to his room and grasped the doorknob to push the door open. Only he did not turn the knob quite far enough, and the door stood firm.

In that moment of frustration, Paul had had enough. Before he could think twice, he had given the door a violent kick.

When he closed the door behind him, there was a gaping hole in it.

I was still standing in the kitchen, where I had just uttered my decree. When I heard the crash, an immediate surge of fury welled up inside me.

I'll teach him.

But the Holy Spirit stepped in, silently, unobtrusively, yet urgently, and whispered a word to my heart from Ephesians, chapter six: "Fathers, do not provoke your children to wrath" (Ephesians 6:4 NKJV).

In only a split second, my entire attitude completely changed. A grieving swept over me, and I felt the hot tears of remorse begin to sting my eyes. I walked into the garage, knelt before the Lord, and asked God for forgiveness for what I had done to my son.

Forty minutes later, I walked back out into the hall toward Paul's room. The Holy Spirit had humbled me.

I opened the damaged door, a somber symbol of my own dictatorial authoritarianism. Big words—but big sin. Paul was still sitting on the edge of his bed, elbows on knees, head in hands. Forty minutes after our angry exchange, there were still tears in his eyes.

I sat down beside him.

"Paul, I sinned against you," I said quietly. "I'm your dad, but I provoked you to wrath. I want you to know that I love you, and I ask you to forgive me for my sin."

I promised him the credit card and the keys.

"You go to camp."

He went.

It was at that camp that God took hold of Paul's life. He was called to a ministry at that youth camp and has served in Christian ministry ever since.

God's admonition to fathers is not to provoke our sons and daughters to wrath, but to raise them in the nurture and admonition of the Lord.

When we wrong our children, it is not a sign of weakness to ask for their forgiveness.

It is evidence of moral strength.

THE CHALLENGE

+ Fathers who punish their children for doing wrong when they haven't first taught them how to do right are themselves wrong.

+ Children may not always listen to you, but they will always imitate you.

+ A father is only qualified to lead his family to the degree he is willing to serve them.

+ Men are stewards, not owners, of their children. In God's plan, a man's stewardship can never be relinquished.

THE WORD

Fathers, provoke not your children to wrath: but bring them up in the nurture and admonition of the Lord.
Ephesians 6:4 KJV

Fathers, do not exasperate your children; instead, bring them up in the training and instruction of the Lord.
Ephesians 6:4

Fathers, don't scold your children so much that they become discouraged and quit trying.
Colossians 3:21 TLB

I have no greater joy than to hear that my children are walking in the truth.
3 John 1:4

28

ONLY YOUNG ONCE....?

You are only young once, but you can live immature for a lifetime.

I have carried the message that *"Manhood and Christlikeness are synonymous"* literally around the world. In one meeting, a member of the House of Lords in England exclaimed aloud, "I have never heard such a truth before."

One of the truths that resounds in every culture worldwide is the problem of immature and irresponsible men. Men who just refuse to grow up, clinging childishly to their youth.

God commends childlikeness but scorns childishness. The whole purpose of the fivefold ministry gifts in the church is to enable men to mature, to grow up into the stature of the measure of being Christlike (Ephesians 4:13).

What's the difference between government bonds and men? Bonds mature.

Sure, that's a male-bashing joke, but the meaning is not lost on us. Men don't automatically mature as we grow older.

Maturity doesn't come with age but begins with the acceptance of responsibility.

The first Adam in the garden of Eden refused to accept responsibility for his actions, while the last Adam—Jesus Christ—accepted responsibility for the actions of the entire world.

Therein is the difference between men. At one end of the spectrum, some can't even accept responsibility for their own actions. At the other end are men who not only accept responsibility for themselves but also for their family and the world for which Christ died. The first is an immature and childish man. The last is a mature and Christlike man of covenant.

Every man has the option to be a male, a man, or a covenant man.

The Peter Pan syndrome—the refusal to grow up—is not an aberration or addiction. It is an abnormality.

To accept responsibility, make wise decisions, and serve those you love are three marks of a man. Irresponsibility, foolishness, and insensitivity are blemishes on a man's character.

A childish man is an immature man.

Some men are more mature at seventeen than others are at forty-seven. As long as a man is in denial, refusing to accept responsibility for his own actions, he cannot find help for his problems. Neither can he be responsible for success until he is willing to accept responsibility for failure.

There is a vast difference between being childlike and childish. Youth has its virtue, old age has its glory, but just acting like a child all your life is another matter. Women love raising children but not husbands.

When I teach this, I make the statement that when a man acts like a child, it forces his wife to act like his mother. A more serious problem is that you can't make love to your mother. Reaction to that is almost always a loud groan.

However, it is true. When a man's childishness causes problems in his intimate relationship, he usually blames it on his wife, saying she is frigid or doesn't understand him. The truth is, she understands him too well.

Grown men tell their wives, "It's my way or the highway." Childish!

Paul's wisdom is for all men: "When I was a child, I spoke as a child, I understood as a child, I thought as a child; but when I became a man, I put away childish things" (1 Corinthians 13:11 NKJV).

The transition from childishness to manhood, from irresponsibility to responsibility, from immaturity to maturity, is a passage that every man must make.

THE CHALLENGE

+ Being a male is a matter of birth. Being a man is a matter of choice.

+ Consistency, decisiveness, and strength are what God wants, and what women and children need, from men.

+ A man's inconsistencies are usually testimonies to his immaturity.

+ It is one thing to accept responsibility for self, another to accept responsibility for others.

THE WORD

When I was a child, I spoke as a child, I understood as a child, I thought as a child; but when I became a man, I put away childish things.

1 Corinthians 13:11 NKJV

Until we all reach unity in the faith and in the knowledge of the Son of God and become mature, attaining to the whole measure of the fullness of Christ.

Ephesians 4:13

29

THE BLAME GAME

Every man must answer for his own actions.

Self-justification has been the error of humanity since Adam blamed Eve.

President Harry Truman made himself a folk hero with this sign on his Oval Office desk: "The buck stops here." It became the mark of his leadership.

Buck-passing is the colloquial term for "self-justification." Self-justification means "making yourself right in your own eyes." The pattern for self-justification was set in Eden, and it is still alive today.

Adam sinned, then hid himself from God. When God called, Adam answered, "I was afraid because I was naked; and I hid myself" (Genesis 3:10 NKJV).

Guilt, fear, and hiding is the sequentially ordered result of sin. It was established millenniums ago in Eden and is still the same today.

No man can live with guilt. It is a killer. Guilt weighs heavily and leads to fear. So, men still hide. They try to escape. Escape reality. Escape God. Escape responsibility. They do it with philosophy, drugs, alcohol, and pleasure-seeking.

But getting rid of guilt by any of these methods is just being made right in your own eyes. It's self-justification. Buck passing. Adam wrote the "how-to" pattern for trying to get rid of guilt and set it for all men, from then until now.

"Did you take of the tree?" God asked Adam.

"The woman made me do it."

Place it on someone else. Easy. Take your guilt, give it to another by putting the blame on them, and you are free. Just pass the buck.

Eve learned from Adam. Asked if she had taken the fruit, she answered according to pattern: "The devil made me do it."

Eve made herself right in her own eyes by placing the blame on the devil.

Self-justification has been the error of humanity since Adam blamed Eve, and Eve blamed the devil.

Men today practice as a science what Adam and Eve practiced as a desperate experiment. Modern man blames the woman as if that is the way it should be.

Wrong.

Every man must answer for his own actions. And he must answer to God alone. That is why Calvary, where Christ died, is so important. It is the only place in the world where sin can be placed and forgiveness from God received. The only place where guilt can be released.

Tragic consequences are left on society by men who still try to cover their mistakes, errors, and sins. Men who would rather let their marriage die than admit their sin and give it new life. Men who would rather let their business collapse than confront failure and restore it. Men who would rather let their children flee in frustration than come to grips with their own shortcomings and renew those ragged relationships. Men who would rather blame God.

God asked Adam: "Did you take of the tree I told you not to?" God was dealing with Adam as a Father to a son. God wanted Adam to be a man: "Answer the question. Did you, or didn't you?"

"The woman *you* gave me, she gave me of the tree, and I did eat," Adam answered—and failed the test of manhood. Adam blamed God for his trouble. Adam refused to accept responsibility for his actions. Adam's reply set the course for mankind. Cover yourself—blame somebody.

God is not the cause of our problems, but he is our only solution. To blame God for what men do is to deny our source of help. Real men accept responsibility for their own actions and find help from God in their time of need.

Real men accept responsibility. God forgives and then helps the man who seeks after him.

THE CHALLENGE

- Adam was the first man not to accept responsibility for his sin, but he was certainly not the last.

- When it comes to sin, the difference between human wisdom and divine wisdom is that divine wisdom faces it and repents, while human wisdom wants to cover it up.

- Self-righteousness begins with self-justification.

- Guilt is a killer. It burdens the conscience, weighs on the spirit, and deadens relationships.

THE WORD

Every way of a man is right in his own eyes, but the Lord weighs the hearts.   Proverbs 21:2 NKJV

A man may ruin his chances by his own foolishness and then blame it on the Lord!   Proverbs 19:3 TLB

Whoever hides his transgressions will not succeed, but whoever confesses and forsakes them will find mercy.   Proverbs 28:13 ISV

30

SUCCESS RESTS ON ONE THING

Success is the antidote to failure.

Accepting responsibility for failure is the substance on which success rests. No man can be responsible for success unless he is first willing to accept responsibility for failure.

True in business, marriage, and all of life.

The popular notion is that maturity comes with age. Not true. You get old with age. Maturing comes by the acceptance of responsibility. The ability to accept responsibility and overcome failure is a measure of mature manhood.

God never planned a failure. God never builds anything on a negative, always on a positive. And God never ends anything on a negative.

Our lives were never planned for failure. You may have failed, but you are not a failure.

To live in failure and with failure is not only stupid but immature. Facing failure is tough. But living with it is tougher. Exercising faith in God and gaining an understanding of his Word helps us to face failure.

In the Bible, Joseph plummeted from the heights to the depths, being sold by his brothers, stuck in a pit, a slave in Potiphar's house, then an inmate in a prison. Joseph's faith in God led him to ultimate success as second-in-command over all of Egypt. When Joseph was reunited with his brothers, he said, "You meant evil against me; but God meant it for good" (Genesis 50:20 NKJV).

God has arranged for men to take what was meant for evil and submit it to God, and let his transcendent glory change it into good.

The prophet Daniel's life of devotion to his beliefs prepared him for the lions' den (Daniel 3). The three Hebrew children would never have taken their stand in the fire without being deeply rooted in God's Word by faith (Daniel 6). We don't know how strong our faith is until we're tested. God tests us in order to prove us. In the end, he sets us up for success, not failure.

Legendary basketball coach John Wooden said, "Failure to prepare is preparation for failure."

True in sports. True in life.

You must prepare for the testing time. Spend time in God's Word. Strengthen your faith now, not when you need it. It's like insurance. You don't buy it after you become ill. You buy it when you're well.

Now is the time. Turn your belief into faith by acting upon it.

Success is the antidote to failure.

Don't despise failure—if it comes, use it as a catalyst for success. Better to try something and fail than to quit and succeed in doing nothing. That's why successful men do not fear failure—each failure brings them closer to success. Successful men are not those who never fail but those who never quit.

Failure is not final.

If you have suffered failure—job loss, divorce, bankruptcy, loss of friendship—when you commit and submit that to Christ, know this: there will be a resurrection for you. Just as the sting of death is removed by the resurrection, so the sting of failure is removed by success.

Don't throw away your failures.

Use them as the underpinning for right decisions today and tomorrow.

Success is born out of failure.

THE CHALLENGE

+ You never know the joy of success until you have experienced the sorrow of failure.

+ Most successful businessmen have "died" through failure before succeeding.

+ Everything in life has value. There is value in failure. What seemed worthless yesterday may have great value tomorrow.

+ Yesterday's sorrows, failures, or tragedies become the basis for something new and better today, making for a more wonderful tomorrow.

THE WORD

Let your character [your moral essence, your inner nature] be free from the love of money [shun greed— be financially ethical], being content with what you have; for He has said, "I WILL NEVER [under any circumstances] DESERT YOU [nor give you up nor leave you without support, nor will I in any degree leave you helpless], NOR WILL I FORSAKE OR LET YOU DOWN OR RELAX MY HOLD ON YOU [assuredly not]!" So we take comfort and are encouraged and confidently say, "THE LORD IS MY HELPER [in time of need], I WILL NOT BE AFRAID. WHAT WILL MAN DO TO ME?"

Hebrews 13:5–6 AMP

Not as though I had already attained, either were already perfect: but...I press toward the mark for the prize of the high calling of God in Christ Jesus.

Philippians 3:12, 14 KJV

Blessed is the man who walks not in the counsel of the ungodly, nor stands in the path of sinners, nor sits in the seat of the scornful.   Psalm 1:1 NKJV

31

THE MOST DESIRABLE THING

Every need in human life is met through wisdom.

Knowledge, understanding, wisdom—all are vital to life. Of these three, God calls wisdom "the principal thing" (Proverbs 4:7 KJV).

"Get wisdom!" the Bible declares (Proverbs 4:5).

Nothing we seek can compare with wisdom. "For wisdom is more precious than rubies, and nothing you desire can compare with her" (Proverbs 8:11).

But be warned—there are two different types of wisdom. Divine wisdom. Human wisdom.

"The wisdom that is from above is first pure, then peaceable, gentle, willing to yield, full of mercy and good fruits, without partiality and without hypocrisy" (James 3:17 NKJV).

That is divine wisdom.

The characteristics of divine wisdom stem from the character of God—peaceable, merciful, without hypocrisy. The results of godly wisdom are a long, good life, riches, honor, pleasure, and peace (Proverbs 3:17).

In other words, *godly wisdom provides for a man's total needs.*

Divine wisdom is the key to achievement in every area of life. Think of wisdom as it relates to your marriage, decisions, financial problems, or health. There is no area in your life that will not benefit from wisdom. Wisdom is the key to all the challenges confronting you.

The one true source of wisdom is God's Word. Christ came as God's Word in human form. Through Christ, God freely gives us wisdom. Jesus has "become for us wisdom" (1 Corinthians 1:30). Christ enables us to know the manifest wisdom of God.

God admonishes us to ask him for wisdom and promises to give it generously without finding fault or looking for an excuse not to answer our request (James 1:5).

The gap between godly wisdom and human wisdom is unfathomably wide.

Human wisdom "is earthly, sensual, demonic. For where envy and self-seeking exist, confusion and every evil thing are there" (James 3:15–16 NKJV).

Our troubled world—filled with envy, strife, and difficulty—is the product of human wisdom.

In our earthly wisdom, we have reordered our value system according to our lusts. Man looks at his vast technological advancements and thinks he is wise. He teaches philosophies that provide questions but no answers. He espouses a science that mocks God yet is unable to provide anything but unproven theories for how the world began or maintains itself.

"Has not God made foolish the wisdom of the world?" (1 Corinthians 1:20).

It is true that since Eden, man has not improved in his nature. We may have more technical knowledge, but our nature is still the same.

James asks pointedly, "Who is wise and understanding among you?...Do not boast and lie against the truth" (James 3:13–14 NKJV).

The sophisticated spirit of the modern era based on human wisdom brings discord, hurt, and eventual ruin. Human wisdom taught a generation of world leaders to believe that the deeper your debt, the better off the economy will be. This philosophy has brought America to the brink of economic ruin.

What is the prerequisite for acquiring godly wisdom? The Bible tells us, "The fear of the LORD is the beginning of wisdom" (Proverbs 9:10). To fear God means, in reverent awe, to acknowledge him for who he is, in all his power and majesty.

The human wisdom that sends us out to do our own thing is not the wisdom that will lead us into our Canaan land.

You can never maximize your potential until you have received God's wisdom.

Any man can get it. Every man needs it.

THE CHALLENGE

+ Three things every man needs: God's favor, wisdom, and courage.

+ Begin to operate in the realm of divine wisdom rather than human wisdom.

+ Good advice is based on human wisdom. Godly counsel is based on the wisdom of God's Word.

+ Wisdom gives a strategy for victory that results in the glory of achievement.

THE WORD

How does a man become wise? The first step is to trust and reverence the Lord!   Proverbs 1:7 TLB

If any of you lacks wisdom, you should ask God, who gives generously to all without finding fault, and it will be given to you.   James 1:5

Wisdom shouts in the streets for a hearing. She calls out…to everyone in all the land:…"Come here and listen to me! I'll pour out the spirit of wisdom upon you and make you wise."   Proverbs 1:20–21, 23 TLB

32

JOINT-HEIRS FOR LIFE

Your wife is every bit as worthy of consideration, appreciation, and affection as you think you are.

While general manager of a Christian television station, it fell my lot to fire a young man.

Tom had all the ingredients for great success. As an executive with the station, he had the expertise to become successful. But he wasn't.

Tom had worked in many areas of ministry—and failed each time. Now he had failed at the television station. The dismissal came as no surprise.

"I don't know what to say to you, Tom," I said. "The only thing that I can think is that, for some inexplicable reason, you are not getting answers to your prayers."

Tom acknowledged that prayer had become very difficult. He admitted that the only time he ever prayed anymore was when called on in Christian meetings.

He had not yet made the vital connection between this lack in his life and the struggle he had on the job.

But Tom was gracious. He and his wife, Sue, invited my wife and me to dinner a few days later. That's when the puzzle began to come together.

Sue set a lovely table. I commented on it, and told her that we were appreciative of the invitation to dinner.

"Yes, it sure is great to have you for dinner tonight," Tom interjected playfully. "We'll get a good meal for a change."

Nancy and I glanced at each other but maintained the conversation. A few minutes into the meal, Sue slipped out to the kitchen. As she returned, I noticed her pleasant smile. But at the same moment, her husband quipped, "You know, my wife's from Arkansas—she only wore shoes because you're here."

Sue reddened but kept smiling.

Dinner proceeded, and the frequency of Tom's little barbs increased. Throughout the meal he kept making her the butt of his humor. Eventually, the nervous laughter fell into awkward conversation, but he did not let up.

Tom thought he was being humorous. He was the only one who thought so.

As I sat in that house, I realized why Tom was not a success...why he had such trouble praying...why he was not experiencing the blessings of God. The apostle Peter wrote that if a man doesn't treat his wife as a partner and joint-heir, his prayers will not get ready answers (1 Peter 3:7).

Tom was ignoring this stern admonition. Because of that, Tom was not getting answers to his prayers. Since his prayer life was ineffective, he was failing. And without prayer, even his faith had grown weak.

Your wife must be your joint-heir, every bit as worthy of consideration, appreciation, and affection as you think you are.

Tom is not alone in his sin. The syndrome is epidemic. *Man demeaning his wife* is one of the classic social sculptures of our age. Making his wife the scapegoat for his own failures and the object of his ridicule.

I thought of Sue's background, so different from Tom's. Instead of patiently explaining matters to her, he put her down, even in front of others.

What Tom needed to do—and what *every man* needs to do who is like Tom—was to take Sue someplace and open his heart to her, ask her forgiveness, and let their relationship be healed.

Tom needed to repent to save his marriage. And he needed to change so the string of failures in his life could be broken. Then the pattern of his life and marriage could be remade.

Repentance repairs and rebuilds.

THE CHALLENGE

- Men, don't justify yourself in your own eyes by making your wife a scapegoat.

- Many men blame the boss because they don't get the promotion, or blame the guy in the next office who snatched that job away, when the real reason can be found in their own lives.

- Men are failing, stumbling, struggling, and falling short because they are not treating their wives as joint-heirs.

- Spend the time to list the attributes of the wife God gave you. Thank God for each one.

THE WORD

You husbands must be careful of your wives, being thoughtful of their needs and honoring them as the weaker sex. Remember that you and your wife are partners in receiving God's blessings, and if you don't treat her as you should, your prayers will not get ready answers. 1 Peter 3:7 TLB

I will try to walk a blameless path, but how I need your help, especially in my own home, where I long to act as I should. Psalm 101:2 TLB

You flood the LORD's altar with tears. You weep and wail because he no longer looks with favor on your offerings or accepts them with pleasure from your hands. You ask, "Why?" It is because the LORD is the witness between you and the wife of your youth. You have been unfaithful [treacherous] to her, though she is your partner, the wife of your marriage covenant.

Malachi 2:13–14

Without faith it is impossible to please God.

Hebrews 11:6

33

A MIRROR IMAGE

While men look for better methods, God looks for better men.

No one can see a thing with the lights out. In a dark room, trying to walk around, you bump into everything and never know what you hit. Turn on the light, though, and it becomes clear. You can walk safely through it all.

The man who is spiritually dark can't see the nose on the front of his spiritual face. Jesus is the light. In the light of his Word, we see ourselves. The Holy Spirit illumines the truth, and the truth makes us free. God's Word is truth, and his Spirit is the Spirit of truth.

God is not indifferent to your needs. It was because of our needs that Jesus Christ came into this world. It is the men who say they have no needs for whom God can do nothing.

God loves you. God wants your good. God wants your life to be lived to the maximum.

Today, more than ever before in history, men need to recognize how God originally made them to be and earnestly endeavor to let God recreate their manhood in the image of Christ.

Adam was created in the image of God. His was the example of manhood. When that manhood was marred by sin, Jesus Christ came as the "last Adam" to restore the image to men once again.

Christ came as the "express image" of God, to reveal his grace and truth. As Jesus revealed the glory of God, he told you and me that we could be "born again" and receive the very nature of God into our spirits. We could have our minds renewed and our hearts regenerated. From there, our entire life would be so changed that old things pass away and all things become new (2 Corinthians 5:17).

Without Jesus Christ, man is unable to be restored to the image of God as his workmanship, to his glory. With Jesus, it is being done for us today.

With the new image of manhood stamped on our minds, our behavior, attitudes, and desires all become new. We are "new creations" with new motivations for our lives.

Just as Jesus Christ is the head of the church and brings his salvation and solutions, he can do the same through you to your family (Ephesians 5:23). You are the channel. Your family looks to you first. To try to escape from that responsibility is to hide from God. To refuse to acknowledge the need is to avoid reality.

God is looking to you, as a man, to provide leadership. God has given his Word. And by his own Spirit, he has given the perfect tool—divine wisdom. With the Word and wisdom, he expects you to find the solutions.

Such is the challenge of manhood: To know God. To know yourself. To know your family.

The late Christian statesman E. M. Bounds wrote, "Men are God's methods. While men look for better methods, God looks for better men."

God is looking for men who mirror the image of Christ.

What about you?

THE CHALLENGE

+ God gave all Christian men a guide for themselves and their families.

+ God created man in his image. Today men are trying to create God in their image.

+ It is the men who say they have no needs for whom God can do nothing.

+ The Holy Spirit illumines the truth, and the truth makes us free.

THE WORD

Jesus said, "I am the Light of the world. So if you follow me, you won't be stumbling through the darkness, for living light will flood your path."

John 8:12 TLB

But when he, the Spirit of truth, comes, he will guide you into all the truth. He will not speak on his own; he will speak only what he hears, and he will tell you what is yet to come.

John 16:13

The Son is the radiance of God's glory and the exact representation of his being, sustaining all things by his powerful word. After he had provided purification for sins, he sat down at the right hand of the Majesty in heaven.

Hebrews 1:3

Do not conform to the pattern of this world, but be transformed by the renewing of your mind. Then you will be able to test and approve what God's will is— his good, pleasing and perfect will.   Romans 12:2

Therefore, if anyone is in Christ, the new creation has come: the old has gone, the new is here!
                                        2 Corinthians 5:17

34

TENDER AND TOUGH

Balance is the key to life.

I was invited to appear on a national Christian broadcast by a husband-and-wife team to talk about ministering to men. During the interview, I mentioned the principle that *balance is the key to life.*

"Because balance is the key to life," I said, "men must learn to be both tender *and* tough."

The female cohost reacted immediately to the word "tough," and she said so.

"My husband would never be tough with me," she insisted. "And if he were, I wouldn't like it."

"Nevertheless," I countered diplomatically, "the man must be the leader in the home, and sometimes that requires toughness. Not roughness, but toughness."

The point stands. Leadership by the man requires toughness as well as tenderness.

The balance must be kept. With children, the reward must balance the punishment, the caress must balance the discipline, the commendation must balance the correction.

Perhaps years ago, parents, educators, and political leaders erred on the side of toughness as a general rule—but today, it is the softness that is killing us. That is why *balance is the key to life.*

Discipline requires toughness.

Being tough is not being hard. It is being tough enough to face reality, to confront truth, and to embrace it even at your own expense. To be tough is to be a disciplined man.

A friend of mine was retained to examine a failing business and make recommendations for a turnaround. I'm sure the business owner wasn't prepared for the findings.

The owner's problems were his relatives. He had hired many of them to work for him, but they weren't producing. Financially, his relatives were killing him. But because of the intricacy of the relationships, he could not discipline or fire them. Heedless of the recommendation, the business was lost. He might still have that business today if he had been tough enough to speak the truth to his relatives—in love.

His tenderness and toughness were out of balance.

Churches can be that way. Even though a staff member has not been productive for years, they are left in a position through sentiment. If we fail to act in truth because of sentiment, the consequences can be tragic.

The kingdom of God is based on truth, not human sentiment.

Jesus was a perfect balance of tender and tough.

He revealed his tenderness in his messages of love, his actions of healing and comforting, his death on the cross. But the same Jesus who swept little children up into his arms gripped that scourge of cords and drove the money changers out of the temple.

Jesus was a fearless leader, defeating Satan, commanding nature, rebuking hypocrites. He had a nobility of character and a full complement of virtues that can be reproduced in us today by the same Holy Spirit that dwelled in him.

God wants to reproduce this manhood in all men. What kind of manhood?

Christlikeness!

Christlikeness and manhood are synonymous.

THE CHALLENGE

+ Discipline requires toughness.

+ Balance is the key to life.

+ The highest good of every individual, man and woman, is to be like Jesus. God has made everything conform to that ultimate purpose—to produce Christlikeness in us—to make us into his own image.

+ The kingdom of God is based on truth, not human sentiment.

THE WORD

A rod and a reprimand impart wisdom, but a child left undisciplined disgraces its mother.

Proverbs 29:15

My son, do not make light of the Lord's discipline, and do not lose heart when he rebukes you.

Hebrews 12:5

If your right eye causes you to stumble, gouge it out and throw it away. It is better for you to lose one part of your body than for your whole body to be thrown into hell.

Matthew 5:29

35

TIME TO LET GO

Externals don't make the man—internals do.

In Newport Beach, California, a marvelous beach sits hard by jetties on both sides of the isthmus. The jetty has been my private closet for prayer, my meditation room, and my counseling chamber.

When a deeply troubled friend flew down from his new home in Oregon, I told him to meet me at the jetty.

Moving to Oregon, Rick told me, had been a mistake. He had gone there just to get away from everything—only to realize when he arrived that "everything" had come with him. He hadn't left anything at all. A strange consternation was boiling within him.

Just a few weeks before, he had been working on a house he was building when he heard this inner voice say, "Let go." Though he had talked to others about it, he did not know what was happening. Then he felt impressed to fly back to California and see me.

"Is it the Holy Spirit speaking to me?" he wanted to know. "Or the devil? Or who?"

The more we talked, the more I realized God was at work in Rick's life. But Rick had yet to realize it.

"I don't know what to do," he said. "I'm not happy with myself, my wife is not happy with me, and my children are unhappy. If something doesn't happen soon, I don't know what I'll do. And then—I keep hearing this voice inside me saying, 'Let go.'"

Rick had confessed Jesus Christ as his Savior several years before, but he had never made a total commitment. Some areas of his life were still under his own control instead of submitted to God. As we talked and prayed together, the light began to dawn.

It became clear that it really was God speaking by his Spirit to Rick's heart. "Let go" meant to release himself totally into God's hands, trusting entirely in him. Rick came to the realization that God was simply saying, "Let go of all your own ways and depend on me in the totality of life."

With that understanding, we prayed. Rick—forsaking his old ways—submitted to the Lordship of Jesus Christ in his life. In that moment, Rick became more of a man than he had ever been before.

Rick learned to bring his plans, his desires, and his sins to Jesus and exchange them for the unique plan for which God had created him and only God could accomplish.

It is God working in us, "both to will and to do for His good pleasure" (Philippians 2:13 NKJV), that brings forth this kind of true manhood in its various dimensions.

Months later, Rick and his wife, Joan, were sitting in my living room talking about ministering to men.

Suddenly, I noticed that Joan was weeping. I asked her why.

"I'm not crying for me," she said. "I'm crying with happiness for the women who are going to experience the same thing we have. Immediately after Rick surrendered to the Lord, things were different.

"Just three days after he returned to Oregon," Joan continued, "our daughter said, 'Mommy, what happened to Daddy? He's different.'"

Rick and Joan—and their children—discovered that the whole home changes when the man changes.

There was nothing magic about the jetty that day. But there was something new in Rick's heart and life. That's where the change was. He had a new attitude, a new approach to life, a new obedience to God.

Rick was beginning to live a maximized life—a life in his Canaan land.

THE CHALLENGE

+ Surrender does not come easily to men. Humility is hard on our pride.

+ Losing ourselves, admitting we don't know everything, is not fun. But it's better than compromise.

+ Redemption—the process started when God gave his best, Jesus Christ. It continues when a man surrenders his life in commitment to the Lord.

+ To walk in God's will for our lives, secure in our manhood and our relationship with Jesus Christ, is our highest good.

THE WORD

Humble yourselves therefore under the mighty hand of God, that he may exalt you in due time.

1 Peter 5:6 KJV

Submit yourselves, then, to God. Resist the devil, and he will flee from you.   James 4:7

Trust in the LORD with all your heart and lean not on your own understanding; in all your ways submit to him, and he will make your paths straight.

Proverbs 3:5–6

So rend your heart, and not your garments; return to the LORD your God, for He is gracious and merciful, slow to anger, and of great kindness; and He relents from doing harm.   Joel 2:13 NKJV

36

STOLEN WATER IS SWEET

Obedience to God brings peace.

Steve and his wife, Gail, are precious friends. Their home is peaceful, joyous, and filled with love, except for one season that nearly cost Steve his marriage, family, profession—and soul.

Steve worked in a culture where flirtation was a daily ritual. But for Steve, what started as flirtation became furtive dating and finally adultery. Ultimately, Steve made the decision to leave his wife and family, and live the sensuous, "glamorous" life. He moved into an apartment with his girlfriend.

The proverb says it best: "'Stolen water is sweet, and bread eaten in secret is pleasant.' But he does not know that the dead are there, that her guests are in the depths of hell" (Proverbs 9:17–18).

Steve lost his peace of heart.

Gail and her daughters were devastated. No peace. Not in him, her, the girls, anywhere.

Obedience to God brings peace. Disobedience brought confusion, pain, and suffering.

But Gail trusted God's Word. Her faith was unshakable. During those agonizing days, she spent hours in counseling and prayer. She studied God's Word to fill her heart with hope and encouraging promise for Steve's recovery, and for the changes necessary in her so she could love, forgive, and find reconciliation.

The day came when Steve was arrested for drunk driving. In jail—like the prodigal son Jesus talked about—Steve came to himself. With deep contrition of heart and genuine sorrow for his sin, he cried from his heart and his cell.

God heard that cry—and forgave Steve. Upon release, Steve asked his wife for forgiveness and to be restored to his home—and bed. It was not easy for either of them. They both had to talk and pray through his guilt and her jealousy, but they did it. And their home was filled with the peace of God once again.

The pattern of the prodigal is: rebellion, ruin, repentance, reconciliation, restoration. Steve experienced them all.

Human sorrow is when we are only sorry for getting caught. Godly sorrow is when we are sorry for the sin and have an earnest desire to be rid of it. Steve had repented with godly sorrow. His relationship was renewed with his family and his God.

Sorrow is one of life's greatest teachers.

It's what comes afterward that makes it all worthwhile.

The good news is that God never stops loving us.

A Sunday school teacher once asked, "Does God love you if you are a thief or a liar?" The children all answered, "No!" Wrong.

God loves thieves, liars, cheats, murderers, addicts, pimps, the pompous, proud, and arrogant—God loves the sinner, though he hates the sin.

When God's Spirit convicts us of sin, it is not to hurt us, even though it produces sorrow in us. It's to cause us to be willing to be separated from sin and its ugliness, so that God can bring his love, grace, peace, and power in greater degree and measure.

God never stops loving. Period. Obedience to a loving God brings peace.

THE CHALLENGE

+ Real men find their resolution from sin through genuine repentance and reconciliation.

+ Come to the Lord with sorrow and leave with joy.

+ You know how much God loves you by how much he gave for you. Christ proved his love by giving himself for us.

+ Repentance is the pivotal point between ruin and reconciliation.

THE WORD

Now no chastening [discipline] seems to be joyful for the present, but painful; nevertheless, afterward it yields the peaceable fruit of righteousness to those who have been trained by it.   Hebrews 12:11 NKJV

But God demonstrates his own love for us in this: while we were still sinners, Christ died for us.

Romans 5:8

Godly sorrow brings repentance that leads to salvation and leaves no regret, but worldly sorrow brings death.   2 Corinthians 7:10

Repent, then, and turn to God, so that your sins may be wiped out, that times of refreshing may come from the Lord.   Acts 3:19

37

SUCCESSFUL DECISIONS

Every successful man I know is decisive.

Nations, businesses, families, women, children all need decision-makers. Decisions are not always right, but they are always decisions. Even no decision is a decision by default.

Years ago, I heard a friend say, "The man who straddles the fence gets hurt when he falls." It's dangerous.

Decision making is one of the marks of a man.

Women desire men to make decisions. Not as dictators, but as leaders. There is a vast difference. Dictators make decisions based on personal preference or selfish gratification. Leaders make decisions based on what is best for others.

Indecisiveness creates instability. Scripture states that the double-minded man is "unstable in all his ways" (James 1:8 NKJV).

Second-guessing reflects a lack of confidence in a decision already made. If a decision is made and it proves to be faulty or wrong, admit it, repent of it, learn from it. God forgives our faulty decisions. We must go on from that point.

If God forgives us, but we do not forgive ourselves, we make ourselves greater than him. Wisely forgetting the past is part of a man's maturing. It is essential to real manhood. Crying over spilled milk, living with regret, carrying past mistakes—are all wrong. Living with mistakes is a mistake in itself.

A friend's skeptical father reacted to the news that his son was going into the ministry.

"If you're going to start, don't stop!" his dad told him. "And if you're going to stop, don't start!" It was a lesson in accountability that my friend never forgot. He followed his call and built a hugely successful ministry in Chicago.

Mediocre men want authority but not accountability. They do not want to be responsible for decisions they make. They resent those who hold them accountable for their decisions and actions. Such men (*and women!*) want the freedom to choose, but not the consequences of their choices. They desire license, not liberty, because liberty has restraints. License has none.

God never gives authority without accountability.

Men have the ultimate responsibility for their decisions. The essence of maturity is the acceptance of that responsibility. And maturity is the essence of manhood.

Decisions determine conduct, character, and destiny.

The discipline of daily devotion to God undergirds successful decisions. The more of God's Word you have in you, the more Christlike you become, and the greater character you develop. The more Word you have in you, the better foundation for making the right decisions.

Men who make disciplined decisions one after another—abiding in the Word, doing God's will—build within themselves a deeply rooted, godly character that overcomes outward circumstances and devilish spirits. We call such people "men of conviction." Decisions are rooted in the character of such men.

Crisis doesn't make the man. It only exposes him for what he already is. It's the character of a man that stands him in good stead in a time of crisis.

Soulish decisions made after the flesh appear to be good but turn to evil. Spiritual decisions made after the Spirit turn out well.

True in business and in marriage.

Men need to remember the decisions of the home are not ours alone. Our wives are our joint-heirs. No man in marriage should live or act independently of his wife.

Decisions must be made on truth, not feelings.

The decisive man breeds confidence.

Decision making. The mark of a real man.

THE CHALLENGE

+ A man's criteria for decision-making are: Is it spiritual? Moral? Ethical? Legal?

+ A real man doesn't make decisions based on the emotion of the moment or the personal gratification he can garner but on the merits of the decision itself.

+ A man who honors God privately will show it by making good decisions publicly.

+ Peace is the umpire for knowing the will of God (Colossians 3:15).

+ Decisions determine your destiny.

THE WORD

And if it seems evil to you to serve the LORD, choose [decide] for yourselves this day whom you will serve.... But as for me and my house, we will serve the LORD.

Joshua 24:15 NKJV

Commit to the LORD whatever you do, and he will establish your plans.   Proverbs 16:3

Trust in the LORD with all your heart and lean not on your own understanding; in all your ways submit to him, and he will make your paths straight.

Proverbs 3:5–6

Every way of a man is right in his own eyes, but the LORD weighs the hearts.   Proverbs 21:2 NKJV

38

OVERCOME YOUR LIONS

God has a strategy to overcome every obstacle.
We find it in his Word.

Lions are fierce–they are the "kings of the jungle." Their roar is so frightening, it literally causes their quarry to freeze with fear, giving the lions opportunity to launch their voracious attack.

Symbolically, the lions in our lives are jealousy, anger, malice, vengeance, greed, strife, spite, drugs, and other assorted enemies of well-being. The lions' den is that pit of persecution or dungeon of depression in which we are held at the mercy of such thoughts, emotions, and habits that would devour us.

Glen had huge lions to overcome when he discovered his wife's adultery by accident. She generally took care of the household accounts. One day, in her absence, he started paying the bills. Noticing something peculiar with the credit card statement, he called to inquire about the charges and where they had been made. The shock of discovering his wife was buying gifts for another man was emotionally paralyzing. The lions of anger, jealousy, hatred, revenge, and even murder roared in his mind and heart.

Recovering his mental and emotional equilibrium, Glen fell on his face on the floor and cried out to God for help and healing from the deep wound of betrayal. As he lay there under the weight of that great agony, something remarkable happened. The weight came off him, almost in a physical sense. Peace came into his heart, rational thought to his mind, and stability to his emotions.

After fasting and praying, he confronted his wife, and she admitted her guilt. In response, he told her, "I want our marriage to be healed. I love you. You are God's gift to me."

They were still far from the communication necessary to resurrect the marriage, but Glen had already withstood his biggest trial. The mouths of the lions raging against him in the den of his mind and heart were stopped. Figuratively, it was as real to him as it was literally to Daniel.

When Glen told me his story, he attributed the change in his life to God's Word. "When I disciplined myself to read the Word, my life changed. What I learned kept me from being destroyed. Since deciding to become a man of God, this is the first sign I've had that I'm really becoming a new person. Before, I would have told her to get out, then tried to find the guy and who knows what else. Thank God for his grace—and the power of his Word."

The Word produced a new spirit in him. It was as daring, bold, and courageous for him to forgive his wife as any heroic act in history. He is one of those men that Daniel prophesied would do exploits because they know their God (Daniel 11:32).

God has a strategy to overcome every obstacle in our lives. We find it in his Word.

To answer God's call, to accept the honorable ministry of Christ, to face adversity, we have to be spiritually strong. For the men who are rooted and grounded in God's Word, the tough days of life ahead will be the greatest opportunities of all time to see God's glory.

Stabilize your emotions with God's love.

Renew your mind with the Holy Spirit.

Establish your heart in God's Word.

Defeat the lions in your life.

THE CHALLENGE

+ Understanding God's Word always comes by way of revelation. God does not explain himself. He reveals himself.

+ God never tires of revealing himself to men, nor do real men tire of discovering God.

+ Real men are Christlike. Secure in their identification with Jesus, acting in faith on God's Word, believing God will perform what he says, they move through life with confidence and face adversity with courage.

THE WORD

The people that do know their God shall be strong, and do exploits.   Daniel 11:32 KJV

I have hidden your word in my heart that I might not sin against you. Praise be to you, LORD; teach me your decrees.   Psalm 119:11–12

Your word is a lamp for my feet, a light on my path.
Psalm 119:105

For everything that was written in the past was written to teach us, so that through the endurance taught in the Scriptures and the encouragement they provide we might have hope.   Romans 15:4

Stand firm then, with…the sword of the Spirit, which is the word of God.   Ephesians 6:14, 17

39

THE SIGN OF THE COVENANT

Sex is made for loving and giving, not lusting and getting.

I was in Washington, D.C., when an investigative reporter interviewed me. Since everything in that city revolves around politics, he was curious about my organization.

"You talk to men all over the country about sex," he said. "What is the name of your political action committee, and what is it doing about public policy matters like abortion?"

"I'm teaching men to refrain from premarital sex and to be faithful to their wives after marriage," I said. "If men do that, you won't need new laws."

"That's impossible!" he said.

"You obviously don't understand the Bible," I said. "And you don't understand the power of God, or you wouldn't say that. I've seen thousands of men, when confronted with truth, respond to it like real men."

In this society—filled with pornography, where lust is glorified, sex is cheap, marriage is portrayed as nothing but a problem but living together is a solution, where a woman is seen as an object to gratify a man's lust—in the midst of this, it is a thrill to see men make decisions to reject that culture and commit themselves to being real men, being Christlike.

God created marriage between a man and a woman as a covenant relationship.

God establishes life through sacred covenants. A covenant is the external evidence of an internal work. God made a covenant with Abraham and established the nation of Israel. God made a covenant with us in Christ and established his body, the Church. In marriage, a man and a woman make a covenant to one another and establish the family. Sex is the sign of that covenant. Sex is sacred because God-ordained covenants are sacred.

God doesn't change the covenants to fit the trends. Including the covenant of marriage.

Sex is the highest physical act of love between a man and a woman. When a man and a woman are joined together in marriage, their spirits become united, and they become "one flesh" (Matthew 19:5). Sex is the physical evidence of their covenant. It is the external evidence of the internal work.

Someone once asked, "Isn't it dishonoring to say that sex can be regarded as sacred?"

Well, who did they think created sex? The devil didn't. Satan is not a creator. He is a counterfeiter, usurper, and thief.

He will counterfeit, usurp, or steal anything that God creates. God creates. Satan counterfeits. Love gives. Lust gets.

Engaging in any sex act outside of marriage is a sin. Engaging in sex when single is fornication. With a member of the opposite sex when one or both are in covenant with another partner, it is adultery. Between two people of the same sex, it is homosexuality. All of these are referred to in the Bible as sin.

Sex wasn't made for lusting and getting. It was made for loving and giving.

The joy of sex for a man is to know you have entered into a holy, covenant relationship with the woman you love through a joyous, exciting, physically pleasing act that seals your covenant. Each time you have sex with your wife, you are once again saying with every fiber of your being that you are in covenant with her, and that you love her.

Sex with guilt holds regret and shame.

Sex without guilt is the greatest pleasure a man will know.

Sex is for marriage.

Sex is sacred to marriage.

THE CHALLENGE

+ God created sex to be enjoyable so the husband and wife would desire it and fulfill God's command to replenish the earth.

+ Treat your wife as a covenant partner and joint-heir in the inheritance of God's blessings.

+ Many marriages start wrong, stay wrong, and end wrong. Often, much of this happens because men do not understand that sex is sacred, or that sex is intended for loving and giving, not for lusting and getting.

+ In a society whose heroes are promiscuous, profane, and pernicious, the influence on young people is damning. Who is teaching young people about sex? As a father, that is your right, your responsibility, your honor, and your joy. Don't let anyone steal it from you.

THE WORD

Therefore, I urge you, brothers and sisters, in view of God's mercy, to offer your bodies as a living sacrifice, holy and pleasing to God.   Romans 12:1

Marriage is honorable among all, and the bed undefiled; but fornicators and adulterers God will judge.
                                                  Hebrews 13:4 NKJV

Flee from sexual immorality. All other sins a person commits are outside the body, but whoever sins sexually, sins against their own body.

1 Corinthians 6:18

It is God's will that you should be sanctified: that you should avoid sexual immorality; that each of you should learn to control your own body in a way that is holy and honorable, not in passionate lust like the pagans, who do not know God.

1 Thessalonians 4:3–5

40

TAKE IT TO THE CROSS

Exchange is the process of life.

The cross of Jesus Christ is the place of exchange. When you embrace the cross, the place of Christ's sacrifice and forgiveness, you leave different from the way you came. *Take it to the cross* is the title and banner under which eternal change takes place in our lives. We take:

+ Guilt—and leave with acquittal
+ Repentance—and leave with faith
+ Sorrow—and leave with joy
+ Sin—and leave with righteousness
+ Stupidity—and leave with wisdom

+ Ignorance—and leave with eternal knowledge

+ Disease—and leave with healing

+ Rejection—and leave with acceptance

+ Impotence—and leave with power

You get the idea. The cross takes an old life and makes it become a new creation in Christ Jesus.

"Therefore, if anyone is in Christ, the new creation has come: the old has gone, the new is here!" (2 Corinthians 5:17).

That means—*take it to the cross!*

The cross is the symbol of Christianity.

God's love is connected to the cross. The cross is God's display of love for the world. It's the place of reconciliation between God and man.

The cross is the place of exchange. It's where sin is exchanged for righteousness, death is exchanged for life, and hell is exchanged for heaven.

The cross is where God's wrath against sin was appeased by Christ's sacrifice, so God could be just in forgiving guilty man.

The cross is the centerline of the Bible.

None of us can live according to God's law because we are lawbreakers by nature. We are all guilty of sins, mistakes, errors. Therefore, we need someone to forgive us of our lawbreaking. The law shows us that we are sin-sick by nature. We are in need of a cure. The cure is the free gift of salvation in Christ Jesus. The cure is at the cross.

The cross is where Jesus triumphed over principalities and powers. It's the place where Satan's power is broken.

At the cross, we are crucified to the world, and the world is crucified to us. The cross is where you die to self and sin. To omit the cross is to make Christianity just like any other religion on the face of the earth.

It is the devil's purpose to keep men like you and me from "taking it to the cross." However, Jesus knew—"No cross, no crown!" He knew that the only way to redeem sinful man was by his sacrificial death upon the cross. Only through his redemptive offering could you and I be forgiven of our sins and enter into a covenant relationship with God through Jesus Christ.

No greater sacrifice can be made than that which Christ made at the cross. Jesus said, "Greater love hath no man than this, that a man lay down his life for his friends" (John 15:13 KJV).

Then he proved it by laying down his life for us on Calvary's cross.

The cross is the source of man's greatest glory and Satan's worst defeat.

Sin is exchanged for righteousness.

Death is exchanged for life.

Take it to the cross.

THE CHALLENGE

+ Jesus' cross was to do the will of God at the expense of himself. Our cross is to do the will of God at the expense of ourselves.

+ Our salvation was not bought with corruptible things such as silver and gold but was purchased by the precious blood of Jesus.

+ The symbol of Christianity is not the manger nor the empty tomb, but Calvary's cross.

+ The cross is the culminating place of worship. First an altar, then the tabernacle, the temple, and finally Calvary.

THE WORD

But God forbid that I should boast except in the cross of our Lord Jesus Christ.   Galatians 6:14 NKJV

And being found in appearance as a man, [Jesus] humbled himself by becoming obedient to death— even death on a cross!   Philippians 2:8

God made him who had no sin to be sin for us, so that in him we might become the righteousness of God.
2 Corinthians 5:21

The thief does not come except to steal, and to kill, and to destroy. I have come that they may have life, and that they may have it more abundantly.
John 10:10 NKJV

41

VIDEO DADDY

Images are more powerful than words.

The most powerful thing that can be done in life is to create an image. The next most powerful thing is to destroy an image.

If you can change an image, you can change a behavior.

The images in our mind create the motivations for our behavior. We become the images we have of ourselves. And we treat others according to the images we have of them.

Videos and advertising have been creating and destroying images of manhood for decades, with dangerous results.

Our youths have been traumatized by the "video daddy."

Bart Simpson's cartoon dad, Homer—foolish, weak, bumbling—is outsmarted by his loud-mouthed son. He is the picture of manhood for millions of American children. In its perversion, an image of manhood is stamped on the minds of our youth that results in resentment, derision, anarchy, and mockery.

An exasperated father sat across from me and asked, "What's a man to do?" His son was becoming a real problem. He thought he had been a good father, but he just could not understand his son's attitude. After a long conversation, it became clear that this father was only one of thousands of men in our world today who have become subject to forces they should have controlled.

This father needed to understand the power of images. It was his responsibility to exercise some control over the images that were set before his son. By permitting his son to watch everything that came up on every screen, he was allowing outside forces to create an image of authority in his son's mind.

Those video caricatures became modern-day role models. When the son saw a flaw or weakness in his father, he identified him with the image stamped on his mind via technology. He transferred an image like a "Homer Simpson" to his own father, and then reacted with the same resentment or disdain that he had for the fictional authority figure.

Parents may remain perplexed over their children's behavior until they understand the power of images—now accessible on thousands of streamed venues.

Our youth have been affected by it.

How can we change these negative images?

By letting God renew the images in our minds and in our families.

But—wait a minute. The "video daddy" can also be a dad in real life, an absentee father.

The "video daddy" represented on a screen, or the one abandoning his family to sit in front of it—*which is worse?*

The greatest addiction in America is not marijuana, cocaine, or opioid pills. It is entertainment technology. And it is not only our children who are addicted.

Today's absentee father is often one who goes to work, comes home, and then sits in front of his computer or cell phone instead of spending time with his wife and children. Instead of being absent physically, it is absenteeism nonetheless—an absence of concern for the family.

A father lounges on the sofa looking down at his cell phone for hours, playing games, watching videos. After desperately crying out for daddy's attention, his children sulk off to play. Soon they are clamoring for their own phones or computer tablets, to be like dad—and mom. Now the whole family is lost in their own video worlds with little time for one another.

This is not a maximized life.

Lead your family. Control the images in your home.

Controlling the images in your home will change the atmosphere of your home.

Be the dad who says, "Turn it off. Let's hang out."

THE CHALLENGE

+ Entertainment technology is like a thief. It steals time. It kills initiative. It destroys relationships.

+ Sociologists say fatherlessness is caused by the immaturity of men. It is a pandemic problem in every nation on the planet.

+ One of the most subtle catastrophes has been the anti-hero syndrome that has eliminated our heroes and left us bereft of role models as strong examples.

+ The best daddy is the one who utilizes technology to make the godly of the land his heroes.

+ Are there godly men left in our land? Despite all that the media has said to the contrary, there are.

THE WORD

And he will turn the hearts of the fathers to the children, and the hearts of the children to their fathers.
Malachi 4:6 NKJV

God created man in His own image, in the image of God He created him; male and female He created them.
Genesis 1:27 NKJV

Just as we have borne the image of the earthy man, so shall we bear the image of the heavenly man.
1 Corinthians 15:49

42

THE ULTIMATE DECISION

Enjoy Canaan land in the totality of your life.

My wife, Nancy, is the one who recognized why some men do not enter their personal Canaan land.

"The Israelites sent spies into the land and believed their negative report instead of the promises of God," she said one night. "I believe it was because of their poor self-image of unworthiness and inferiority. They could not believe God would give them all he had promised.

"That's the way it is with us, too," she continued. "We have to die to that old self-image of ourselves that the world, the devil, and sin have stamped on our hearts and minds. That is why men have to have the new image of Jesus Christ stamped on them instead, so they can go into Canaan land."

Then she added, "Make sure they understand that." My wife. "The loveliest lady in the land."

I've watched men from every walk of life come to our meetings negative and downtrodden and leave filled with the brave and bold nature of Christ. God's commands produce the same result in every man, whoever or wherever he may be.

God can do the same for you.

This six-week journey may have uncovered some things that need to change in your life. Repent of those sins—turn from them—*now*.

If you have never asked Jesus to forgive you of your sins, now is the time, and this is the place. If you believe in your heart that Jesus is Lord, but have never confessed him with your mouth, this is the time to do it.

It is with the heart that man believes and is made *righteous*, and with the tongue, he confesses and is given salvation (Romans 10:10).

So—say these words, aloud, right where you are:

"Right now, without any shame or embarrassment, without any hesitation, in front of everybody I know—family, friends, neighbors—I confess that Jesus Christ is my personal Savior.

"I believe that when I asked him to, Jesus forgave me of all my sins and sent his Spirit into my heart.

"Let the angels rejoice at my words right now because I declare on earth that Jesus Christ is Lord, and I declare it to the glory of God the Father.

"Let the devil tremble at my words! I publicly confess that Jesus Christ is the Son of God, that he came from heaven to earth, was born of a virgin, and lived a sinless life. He went about doing good and healing everybody oppressed by the devil. He went to the cross and died for the sins of the world, after which they laid him in a grave.

"But he rose from the dead. And at this very moment, as I pray, he sits at the right hand of the Father in heaven.

"Right now, because of his Spirit in me, I have his victory over the grave, death, hell, the world, the flesh, and the devil, and I praise him for it.

"Right now, Lord, I ask you to bring miraculous changes into my entire life, believing that you will answer me. I praise you for it now."

Brother, in this confession and prayer, you have just obeyed God. Believe that God will answer your prayer and bring great changes into your mind, heart, soul, body, and entire life. Believe God's promises for you—right now.

Don't let someone else create your world for you. For when they do, they will always make it too small.

God is a big God and has big plans for you.

Enjoy Canaan land in the totality of your life.

Marriage. Parenting. Profession. Finances. Education. In every area of your life.

Be a man.

Live a maximized life.

Christlikeness.

THE ULTIMATE DECISION 185

THE CHALLENGE

+ What you believe about God has the greatest potential for good or for harm in your life.

+ What you believe about God shows what you believe about yourself. In prayer, ask God to show you what you need to change in how you see yourself and him.

+ God's primary purpose is deliverance *to*, not *from*. Deliverance *to* salvation requires deliverance *from* sin.

+ You gain by trading. Trade righteousness for salvation. Trade defeat for victory.

THE WORD

If you declare with your mouth, "Jesus is Lord," and believe in your heart that God raised him from the dead, you will be saved. For it is with your heart that you believe and are justified, and it is with your mouth that you profess your faith and are saved.

Romans 10:9–10

For I am not ashamed of the gospel, because it is the power of God that brings salvation to everyone who believes.

Romans 1:16

For it is by grace you have been saved, through faith— and this is not from yourselves, it is the gift of God— not by works, so that no one can boast.

Ephesians 2:8–9

CLOSING THOUGHT: FIRED UP FOR LIFE

"I was born in the fire and can't stand to live in the smoke."

Edwin and Nancy Cole invested their lives ministering to their community and to people around the world. They went to be with Jesus having courageously fulfilled their earthly mission.

We leave you with a last thought from them—one which shows their deeply held beliefs, attitudes, and is no doubt a key to their dedication to each other and to the Lord.

The life they enjoyed for 54 years of marriage and 50 years of a Christian journey is what they so desperately wanted you to have, too. Because through Christ, you can.

I was in a restaurant with a friend who looked at me and said, "I give you the right to speak into my life. Anything you see that needs to be changed, tell me. Or if I am doing something wrong, please let me know. Some people do it without my permission, but I give you the right because I know you will tell me the truth."

I paused for a long time and then gave him my answer.

"Faded glory."

He stared at me and then inquired, "What do you mean?"

"Don't live in faded glory," I said.

"I don't understand," he said.

"Nancy and I were talking about the early days of our lives, when we were both converted. How we would not miss a church service, prayer meeting, or witnessing on the streets. How the glory of God filled our hearts, and the fire of God burned on the altar of our hearts. Then she said something we have said over the years.

"'Edwin, I was born in the fire and can't stand to live in the smoke.'"

"What has that to do with me?" my friend asked.

"When you started over twenty years ago, the glory of God filled everything you did. You learned how to work, worship, lead, witness, teach, sell—whatever a man must do—and now you are a success, but you are still doing the same things the same way.

"You live a contemporary life of faith, but when people look at you, they see things worn and old. You need to take another look at it so you don't live with faded glory.

"A marriage can be in the same condition. The husband says it is great, and the wife says it is mediocre at best. The wonder, awe, passion, and love have waxed cold. It's not the same. She tries to tell him, but he won't listen.

"Men resting on old, faded glory. Marriage partners that began with blessing, wonder, and gratitude now accept divorce as casually as going to the theater. Businesses where consistency was an aim and purpose when they began, but sameness is now the reason for boredom, half-heartedness, and mediocrity.

"Churches and parishioners who began in the glory of God now live in the afterglow of what once was, talking about the past as if it were the present. Talking about what was but now isn't. Faded glory."

As we left the restaurant, he said he would never forget those words.

I hope you won't, either.

In the Old Testament, after Solomon prayed, the glory of God filled the temple. Time went by, and the temple was still there, but the gold was gone, and brass had been put in its place. A sign of faded glory. What was but now isn't.

Nancy said, "Edwin, let's not just fade away, let's burn out for Jesus."

After retiring, the famous General MacArthur said, "Old soldiers never die, they just fade away."

Fade away—that is the way of the flesh, world, earth, and man—*but not God.*

God's glory never fades. People do.

God's glory is the same yesterday, today, and forever.

Be fired up for your marriage, for your work, for whatever God has called you to do. And be fired up for God *for life.*

Don't live in faded glory.

Live the Maximized Life.

THE CHALLENGE

+ Why miss the best part of your life, which is *today?* Yesterday might be good old days. But today, when filled with God's glory, is the best day of your life.

+ We are to walk in grace but be filled with God's glory.

+ For the men who are rooted and grounded in God's Word, the days ahead will be the greatest opportunity of all time to show God's glory.

+ Nothing can compare with God's glory. All the majesty of all the royalty that ever existed on earth combined cannot compare with a scintilla of the glory of God.

THE WORD

We are not like Moses, who used to put a veil over his face so that the Israelites would not gaze at the end of the glory which was fading away.   2 Corinthians 3:13 AMP

But we all, with unveiled face, beholding as in a mirror the glory of the Lord, are being transformed into the same image from glory to glory, just as by the Spirit of the Lord.   2 Corinthians 3:18 NKJV

We have been born anew into an inheritance incorruptible… and undefiled and that does not fade away, reserved in heaven for you.   1 Peter 1: 3-4 AMP, NKJV

Arise, shine; for your light has come, and the glory of the LORD rises upon you.   Isaiah 60:1

MAJORING IN MEN® CURRICULUM
MANHOOD GROWTH PLAN

Order the corresponding workbook for each book, and study the first four Majoring in Men® Curriculum books in this order:

MAXIMIZED MANHOOD: Realize your need for God in every area of your life and start mending relationships with Christ and your family.

COURAGE: Make peace with your past, learn the power of forgiveness and the value of character. Let yourself be challenged to speak up for Christ to other men.

COMMUNICATION, SEX AND MONEY: Increase your ability to communicate, place the right values on sex and money in relationships, and greatly improve relationships, whether married or single.

STRONG MEN IN TOUGH TIMES: Reframe trials, battles and discouragement in light of Scripture and gain solid footing for business, career, and relational choices in the future.

Choose five of the following books to study next. When you have completed nine books, if you are not in men's group, you can find a Majoring in Men® group near you and become "commissioned" to minister to other men.

DARING: Overcome fear to live a life of daring ambition for Godly pursuits.

SEXUAL INTEGRITY: Recognize the sacredness of the sexual union, overcome mistakes and blunders and commit to righteousness in your sexuality.

THE UNIQUE WOMAN: Discover what makes a woman tick, from adolescence through maturity, to be able to minister to a spouse's uniqueness at any age.

NEVER QUIT: Take the ten steps for entering or leaving any situation, job, relationship or crisis in life.

REAL MAN: Discover the deepest meaning of Christlikeness and learn to exercise good character in times of stress, success or failure.

POWER OF POTENTIAL: Start making solid business and career choices based on Biblical principles while building core character that affects your entire life.

ABSOLUTE ANSWERS: Adopt practical habits and pursue Biblical solutions to overcome "prodigal problems" and secret sins that hinder both success and satisfaction with life.

TREASURE: Practice Biblical solutions and principles on the job to find treasures such as the satisfaction of exercising integrity and a job well done.

IRRESISTIBLE HUSBAND: Avoid common mistakes that sabotage a relationship and learn simple solutions and good habits to build a marriage that will consistently increase in intensity for decades.

JUST A BARTENDER: A captivating story of endurance and victory against overwhelming obstacles. The discovery of a man's identity against the backdrop of slavery, negative forces, and a world in turmoil. Stories that every man will identify with—to discover a new source of strength for himself.

ABOUT THE AUTHOR

Dr. Edwin Louis Cole (1922–2002), known as "the father of the Christian men's movement," was called by God to speak with a prophetic voice to the men of this generation. To that end, he founded the Christian Men's Network, a ministry that majors in men and communicates the reality that manhood and Christlikeness are synonymous. A former pastor, evangelist, missionary, business executive, and denominational leader, Dr. Cole and his wife, Nancy, served the Lord together for more than fifty years. Over four million copies of his books are in circulation in more than forty languages, including his best-selling *Maximized Manhood*. Since his death, his legacy and vision have been carried on by his "sons" in the faith as they reach tens of thousands of men each month via books, videos, and other media.

Read more about the movement he started at CMN.men